A GRAMMAR OF
ENGLISH HERALDRY

A GRAMMAR OF
ENGLISH HERALDRY

BY THE LATE
W. H. ST JOHN HOPE
LITT.D., HON. D.C.L. (DURHAM)

SECOND EDITION

REVISED BY
ANTHONY R. WAGNER
Richmond Herald

CAMBRIDGE
AT THE UNIVERSITY PRESS
1953

CAMBRIDGE UNIVERSITY PRESS
Cambridge, New York, Melbourne, Madrid, Cape Town,
Singapore, São Paulo, Delhi, Tokyo, Mexico City

Cambridge University Press
The Edinburgh Building, Cambridge CB2 8RU, UK

Published in the United States of America by Cambridge University Press, New York

www.cambridge.org
Information on this title: www.cambridge.org/9781107402102

First published 1913
Second edition, reissued 1953
Reprinted 1953
First paperback edition 2011

A catalogue record for this publication is available from the British Library

ISBN 978-1-107-40210-2 Paperback

PREFACE TO THE FIRST EDITION

THIS little book is intended to set forth for students the first principles of English Heraldry in such a manner as will enable them to take an intelligent interest in it and to realize its value as the handmaid of history and art.

To this end the original sources of such principles have been appealed to, and every effort has been made to keep clear of the obscurities engrafted in later times upon the older heraldry which have contributed so largely to bring the subject into contempt.

The illustrations have been selected not so much from the pictorial side as to make clear the subject-matter; and they have for the most part been drawn in outline so that students may colour them for themselves.

The author desires to express his thanks to the Rev. E. E. Dorling, M.A., F.S.A., for reading the text when in manuscript and for several valuable suggestions.

W. H. ST J. H.

October 1913

PREFACE TO THE SECOND EDITION

IN revising for the press this little work of the late Sir William St John Hope, my object has been to make as few changes as possible, and I have in fact made alterations only where I have detected a slip or error, or where the progress of later studies has made changes necessary (as, for instance, in the bibliography at the end). If on any point I have found myself differing from the writer on a matter of mere opinion or emphasis, I have naturally made no change.

A. R. W.

August 1952

CONTENTS

LIST OF ILLUSTRATIONS

The blocks of figs. 3, 84, 97, 102–5, 107, and 110–13 have been kindly lent from Hope's *Heraldry for Craftsmen and Designers* by Mr G. J. Hogg, and of figs. 81, 96, 135, 142, 143 by Messrs Bowes and Bowes from *A Concise Guide to the Town and University of Cambridge* by J. W. Clark. Figs. 2, 5, 6, 36–9, 52–73, 77, 85, 94, 116–21, 123–9, 132, 134, 136, 144, 147, 150, 151, 153–64 form part of the illustrations of Mr Oswald Barron's article on Heraldry in the *Encylopaedia Britannica* (11th edition). The remaining illustrations have been drawn by the author, except figs. 4, 88, 95, 98, 106, 108, 109, 114, 115 and 165, which are taken from his *Stall-plates of the Knights of the Order of the Garter, 1348–1485*.

CHAPTER I

DEFINITIONS AND ORIGIN OF HERALDRY

HERALDRY, or Armory as it was anciently called, was in the first place a kind of picture-writing to distinguish a man from his fellows. Quite possibly it originated in such games as children still play, where one pretends to be a bear, another a wolf, another a lion, and so on. From this it was but a step to the painting or tattooing of a device or totem upon a man's breast, and as soon as defensive weapons had been invented, to the transfer and repetition of such figures on shields and targets. This fashion of adorning shields with devices of all kinds has existed from very early times, and any series of Greek vases or Roman monumental sculptures (such as those on Trajan's Column) will furnish examples. Quite a gallery of distinctive emblems may be seen upon the banners and shields of the English and the Normans in the famous Bayeux Stitchwork; but it is clear that at the time of the Norman Conquest such devices did not follow any definite system, and there was nothing in the nature of descent from father to son such as arose later.

During the twelfth century a systematic treatment of the devices on shields gradually grew up, and by the end of it had become crystallized. Gilbert of Clare, who died in 1152, used between 1138 and 1146 a seal with the well-known cheverons of his house (fig. 1); and the three lions or leopards which are still the arms of the King of England (fig. 2) had become so as early as 1177, when they occur on a seal used by John the son of Henry II, as Lord of Ireland. Much about this time there are other indications of the general growth of systematic bearings, and owing probably to the influence of the Crusades, by the beginning of the thirteenth century heraldry had become a recognized science. So many armorial bearings, too, had now been invented as to necessitate the entering of them for reference on long rolls of parchment.

Fig. 1. Clare
(*Gold three cheverons gules*)

Fig. 2. England
(*Gules three gold leopards*)

These rolls of arms, as they are called, are the most important records available for the study of heraldry. Some consisted at first of rows of painted shields, with the name of the owner written over each shield; in others the arms are merely described, and it is by the comparison of these written rolls with those that are merely pictorial, and with contemporary armorial seals, that the simple language may be learned by which arms were first described.

The oldest descriptions of arms are in French, but at the beginning of King Edward IV's reign heraldic language emerged from the French and took an English form, all save purely technical words being simply translated. The old French names of the colours were, however, generally retained, but *or* became 'gold' and *argent* 'silver'. About 1600, however, the use of *or* and *argent* was resumed.

One of the earliest armorial records consists of a series of shields and banners painted on the margins of a manuscript of the *Historia Anglorum* of Matthew Paris, now in the British

2

Museum,[1] written down to the events of the year 1253 by Matthew himself.

Among the oldest pictorial rolls is one in the Heralds' College, now cut up into sections and pasted into a scrapbook. It consists of rows of shields with names over; the date is about 1280.

One of the handsomest pictorial rolls, known as Charles's Roll, belongs to the Society of Antiquaries of London and seems to be a fifteenth-century copy (almost a facsimile) of a late thirteenth-century original.

Of the descriptive rolls the most important is that known from its length as the Great Roll, and is of the reign of Edward II. Further reference to this will be made later.

Rolls that combine picture and description are very rare. A good typical example known as the Stacy-Grimaldi Roll is in the John Rylands Library at Manchester, while the most important is Thomas Jenyns's book in the British Museum.

The value of the pictorial rolls is of course greatly enhanced by their authority for the drawing of arms as well as the colours employed.

Heraldry appears upon seals almost as soon as it became systematized; and about the same time that the earliest rolls were drawn it began to be displayed upon monuments and in association with architecture in buildings. Where monumental heraldry has retained the colouring that was so universally applied to it, the shields are evidence as valuable as the rolls. A beautiful early instance of such shields combined with architecture can be seen in the aisles behind the quire in the abbey church of Westminster (figs. 3 and 101), which aisles can be proved by these very shields to have been built before 1269. Another good series, mostly in pairs to

[1] Royal MS. 14 c vii.

denote alliances, is carved upon the gate-house of Kirkham Priory in Yorkshire, which can thus be shown to have been built between 1289 and 1296. Heraldry plays a prominent part in the nave and presbytery of York Minster, and in part of the nave of St Albans, as well as in many a parish church,

Fig. 3. Shield of the arms of Old France in
Westminster abbey church

like that at Lavenham in Suffolk. A fine array of early Tudor shields and badges is to be seen upon the old prior's gateway at Peterborough. Chimney-pieces have at all times been used for the display of heraldry. Early window glass often contains beautiful coloured shields of arms, as at York, Tewkesbury, Gloucester, and many other places.

Heraldic seals are especially valuable objects of study. They extend in an unbroken and ever-growing series from the close of the twelfth century, at the time that armory was becoming a thing of life, and they were constantly being engraved for men of every rank, and even for ladies (fig. 4),

4

Fig. 4. Seal of Cecily Nevill, wife of Richard duke of York
and mother of King Edward IV, 1461

5

who bore and used arms, and for cities and towns, and other corporate bodies (like the monastic houses, the halls and colleges at the universities, and the London livery companies) entitled to have seals.

Moreover, since seals were produced under the direction of, and continually being used by their owners, the heraldry on them has a personal interest of the greatest value, as showing not only what arms the owners bore, but how they were intended to be seen. Seals were engraved too by the foremost craftsmen of the time; and owing to their small size, which rarely exceeds that of a crown piece and is usually much less, they present in a concentrated form everything that is beautiful and delightful in heraldry, all through the days when people revelled in it and played with it.

CHAPTER II

THE GRAMMAR OF HERALDRY

INASMUCH as nearly all early heraldry is displayed upon shields it is of them that mention must first be made. Banners, and painted or embroidered surcoats or coats-of-arms, occur almost equally early, but as the heraldry upon them is the same as upon the shields, they need not be dealt with until later.

The most notable feature of all early heraldry is its simplicity. Some shields are merely divided into two plain colours by a line down or across the middle, or quartered by a use of cross lines. Others are painted checkerwise, or in bands or stripes of alternate colours. Others again are crossed by single bands with birds or beasts or flowers of some kind disposed above and below. Or one, two, three, or more such objects by themselves may be represented, like the three leopards in the arms of the King of England and the six eagles of Piers Gaveston.

Another noteworthy feature is the simplicity of the colouring. The so-called primary colours, red, yellow, and blue, were most in use, but white and black are nearly as common. Of the secondary colours green, oddly enough, is comparatively rare, as is purple; while orange was not used at all in medieval times, apparently because no stable pigment for it was known. Of these tinctures, five were reckoned as colours: red, blue, black, green, and purple. Yellow was usually represented, as might be expected, by gold, and white similarly by silver, and both were accordingly reckoned as metals. Two furs also occur in early heraldry: the familiar black tails on white, known as ermine (fig. 5);

and an alternating arrangement of blue and white patches, imitated from a series of grey squirrels' skins and called vair, from an old French word meaning a skin of various colours (fig. 6). Vair is also often found in other colours, such as black and white, or gold and blue, and was then called vairy. A treatment of ermine with white tails upon black (sable

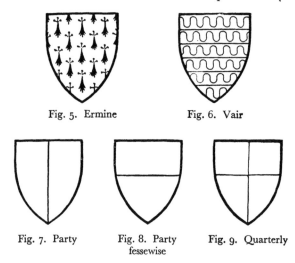

Fig. 5. Ermine   Fig. 6. Vair

Fig. 7. Party   Fig. 8. Party   Fig. 9. Quarterly
fessewise

ermined silver) came into being in the fifteenth century; and later still were invented 'gold ermined sable' and its reverse, 'sable ermined gold'.

Since the simple divisions of the shield possibly gave rise to what are now called the ordinaries, these must now be described.

Shields were divided vertically, or horizontally, or into quarters by a combination of both lines; and described accordingly as 'party' (fig. 7), 'party fessewise' (fig. 8), and 'quarterly' (fig. 9).

8

A division aslantwise from the upper right-hand corner of the bearer was 'party bendwise' (fig. 10), or if from the left-hand corner, 'party bendwise sinister' (fig. 11). A combination of both lines formed 'party saltirewise' (fig. 12);

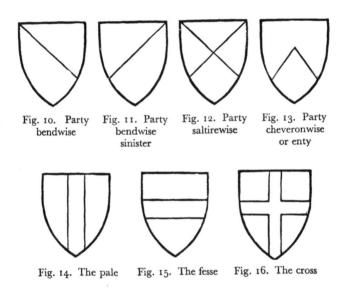

Fig. 10. Party bendwise   Fig. 11. Party bendwise sinister   Fig. 12. Party saltirewise   Fig. 13. Party cheveronwise or enty

Fig. 14. The pale   Fig. 15. The fesse   Fig. 16. The cross

and the lower quarter only of this was 'party cheveronwise' (fig. 13), or 'enty' as it was called in the fifteenth century.

By substituting stripes or bands for these lines there are produced the ordinaries after which they are named: the pale (fig. 14), the fesse (fig. 15), and the cross (fig. 16); the bend (fig. 17), the bend sinister (fig. 18), the saltire (fig. 19), and the cheveron (fig. 20).

To these must be added the chief or head of the shield (fig. 21), and the pile (fig. 22); but in early heraldry there was practically no difference between a chief and party fessewise.

9

Multiples of the ordinaries produced further divisions. Thus an even number of pales gives 'paly' (fig. 23), and a fesse when multiplied becomes 'bars', or 'barry' when

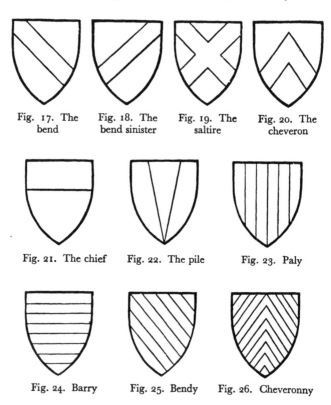

Fig. 17. The bend

Fig. 18. The bend sinister

Fig. 19. The saltire

Fig. 20. The cheveron

Fig. 21. The chief

Fig. 22. The pile

Fig. 23. Paly

Fig. 24. Barry

Fig. 25. Bendy

Fig. 26. Cheveronny

the number is even (fig. 24). A number of bends form 'bendy' (fig. 25), and of cheverons 'cheveronny' (fig. 26), though this is rarely found. Paly with barry form 'checky' (fig. 27), and the crossing of the bendys 'masculy' or 'lozengy' (fig. 28), while the conjunction of quarterly and party saltirewise produces 'gyronny' (fig. 29).

Gyronny was, however, sometimes drawn of six, ten, or even twelve, instead of the more usual eight, pieces, as its divisions were called. Paly, barry, and bendy were also drawn to a limited number of pieces. This was usually six,

Fig. 27. Checky   Fig. 28. Lozengy   Fig. 29. Gyronny

Fig. 30. Pily wavy   Fig. 31. The quarter

but if the shield were a large one the early heralds did not hold themselves to any rule on this point. The number, however, was always even, and should be stated in the blazon if it is more or less than the normal six. 'Buruly' is an old term for apparently an indefinite number of bars.

Fig. 30 represents an early shield of the arms of Gernon, which were *pily wavy of six pieces silver and gules.*

Five other ancient ordinaries were the quarter (fig. 31), now often called a canton, and then drawn somewhat less than a quarter; the scutcheon (fig. 32), or superposition of a smaller shield upon a larger; the orle (fig. 33), false-scutcheon, or pierced-scutcheon; the border (fig. 34); and the flanches, which were always borne in pairs (fig. 35).

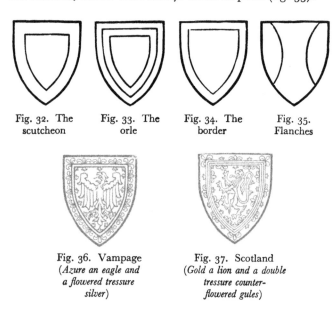

Fig. 32. The scutcheon

Fig. 33. The orle

Fig. 34. The border

Fig. 35. Flanches

Fig. 36. Vampage
(*Azure an eagle and a flowered tressure silver*)

Fig. 37. Scotland
(*Gold a lion and a double tressure counter-flowered gules*)

The curious narrow flowered and counter-flowered orle called the tressure (fig. 36), which figures doubled so prominently in the arms of the King of Scots (fig. 37), was seldom used south of the Tweed.

Further variations of the ordinaries were obtained by the use of other than straight lines, such as: indented (fig. 38); engrailed (fig. 39); and wavy (fig. 40).

But at first, indented and engrailed seem to have been practically the same, and the words interchangeable. Later on came in: battled (fig. 41); ragged (fig. 42); nebuly (fig. 43); and invected (fig. 44).

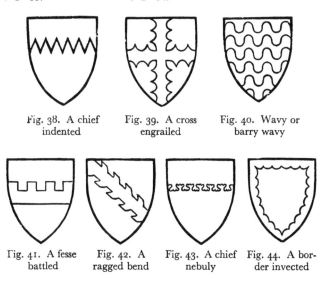

Fig. 38. A chief indented

Fig. 39. A cross engrailed

Fig. 40. Wavy or barry wavy

Fig. 41. A fesse battled

Fig. 42. A ragged bend

Fig. 43. A chief nebuly

Fig. 44. A border invected

'Nebuly' is supposed to represent the edges of clouds, as drawn by the medieval artist, and 'invected' is the reverse of engrailed.

Since French was the 'vulgar tongue' of the Court when heraldry was invented, gold was called *or*, silver *argent*, green *vert*, black *sable*, and purple *purpure*. Red was *gules*, from the Arabic name 'gul' for a red rose. In the same way blue was *azure*, from the Arabic 'lazura', the blue stone called lapis-lazuli.

There has never been any rule as to the tint of a colour, and so long as gules, azure, vert, and purpure can fairly be described as red, blue, green, or purple, the particular shade, whether light or dark, is immaterial.

In connexion with the metals and colours, care was always taken in English heraldry to avoid the placing of a gold object upon silver, or a silver one upon gold, or of a coloured object or bearing upon a coloured field. A few isolated exceptions occur that only serve to prove the rule, and these are so noteworthy from their rarity as to invite enquiry into their meaning. Perhaps this is why the Crusaders devised

Fig. 45. The
Earl Marshal

Fig. 46. Robert
de Reydon

Fig. 47. John
de Chauvant

for the arms of Jerusalem one large and four little gold crosses upon a silver field.

The rule does not however extend to parti-coloured or quarterly fields, nor to fields that are checky, paly, barry, etc. Thus the Great Roll furnishes such examples as a red lion upon a field party gold and vert (fig. 45), a silver leopard upon party gold and gules, and wavy red bars upon party gold and silver; likewise of 'quarterly of silver and sable a bend gold', 'checky silver and gules a cross azure' (fig. 46), 'paly of silver and azure a fesse gules' (fig. 47), and 'buruly of silver and gules three lions of sable'. Other examples show that chiefs and quarters were also excepted from the rule, as well as borders and labels and other differences: 'paly of silver and azure with a chief gules and a golden leopard'; 'barry of six pieces silver and gules with

a quarter gules and a molet of silver in the quarter' (fig. 48);
'quarterly of gold and gules with a border of vair' (fig. 49);
and 'bendy of gold and azure and a label gules'. Arms like
'checky of gold and gules a fesse of ermine', and 'vairy of
silver and sable a fesse of gules', show that the furs came
under the same rule.

The shape of the shield, as will be shown presently, is
a matter of indifference, and its many varieties of form are
merely due to fashion without any heraldic significance; the
ground of it is called the field.

Fig. 48. William
Wasse

Fig. 49. Richard
FitzJohn

An infinite number of arms has been formed by combinations of parti-coloured fields, like barry, paly, or bendy with
ordinaries, and of parti-coloured ordinaries, such as checkered cheverons or fesses, on plain fields. Bends and borders
were often gobony, that is of an alternating series of pieces,
or gobets, of a metal and colour, such as blue and silver,
or gold and sable. Fesses were sometimes placed between
pairs of very narrow bars, called gemells(fig. 50), which also
occur by themselves; and bends between a pair of similar
narrow strips, called cotises (fig. 51). These are often different in colour from the bend, which suggests that they
may have originated in the one bend placed upon another
to be met with in early rolls; but cotises are occasionally
found with other ordinaries like the pale or the cheveron.

When a bend was placed over the other charges in a shield, such as a chief or other ordinary, or a lion or like object, it was originally termed a baston, and was often gobony: it was also usually drawn narrower than a bend (fig. 52). A fesse that zigzagged across the field was called a daunce or

Fig. 50. Geoffrey de la Mare (*Gold a fesse and two gemell-bars azure*)

Fig. 51. Thomas de Peres (*Vert a bend silver and two cotises gold*)

Fig. 52. John Mauleverer (*Gules a chief gold and a baston gobony of silver and azure*)

Fig. 53. Vavasour (*Gold a daunce sable*)

dance, perhaps because its points 'danced' up and down (fig. 53), and cotises were often drawn as zigzags or dancetty.

The blank spaces about an ordinary were filled from the first by devices of every kind, known collectively as charges (figs. 54, 55). A charge or number of charges was also placed on the ordinaries themselves, or both field and ordinary might be charged, or carry charges. Charges were also used alone or in multiple without ordinaries.

For these charges every conceivable creature and inanimate thing was drawn upon: birds, beasts, fishes, reptiles, insects, and parts of them such as heads, limbs, tails, feet, and wings (figs. 56–60); trees, flowers, fruits (fig. 61), and leaves; the sun, moon, and stars; castles, buckles, shells

Fig. 54. Howard (*Gules a bend and six crosslets fitchy silver*)

Fig. 55. John de Pateshulle (*Silver a fesse sable and three scallops gules*)

Fig. 56. *Sable a cheveron silver and three silver owls*. Burton

Fig. 57. *Azure three roach swimming*. Roche

Fig. 58. *Azure three lions' heads rased gold*. Sir Gawayne the good knight

Fig. 59. *Silver three forked tails of lions sable*. Pynchebek

(fig. 63), chaplets (fig. 64), sheaves (fig. 66), sleeves (fig. 67), crosses, crowns, fleurs-de-lis, horse-shoes, etc. Even the writer of the Book of St Albans has to say: 'Bot for to reherce all the signys that be borne in armys as Pecok Pye Ball Dragon Lyon & Dolfyn and flowris and leevys it war to longe a tariyng. ner I can not do hit: ther be so mony.'

A few of these charges like crosses, billets, fleurs-de-lis, scallops, trefoils, and drops, were often used in a diminutive form to powder the field around or about a larger charge (fig. 68).

Arms with party fields were sometimes countercoloured, by interchanging the tinctures, so that the ordinary or charges

Fig. 60 *Gules a pair of gold wings.* Seymour

Fig. 61. *Silver three red apples.* Applegarth

Fig. 62. *Silver three fleurs-de-lis sable.* Bereford

Fig. 63. *Sable a fesse engrailed and three whelk shells gold.* Shelley

Fig. 64. *Silver three chaplets of red roses.* Hilton

Fig. 65. *Azure a silver fleur-de-lis.* John de Tykebi

Fig. 66. *Azure three gold sheaves.* The Earldom of Chester

Fig. 67. *Gold a sleeve or maunche vert.* Thomas de Burnham

Fig. 68. Mounfort (*Silver crusilly gules and a lion azure*)

(or parts of them) overlying the metal were of the colour, and those over the colour of the metal. Several instances occur in the early roll *c.* 1300 called St George's. Thus John de Hudehovile bears 'party gold and azure a saltire countercoloured';

David ap Griffid, 'quarterly gold and azure four leopards countercoloured'; and Philip de Cerne, 'party fessewise silver and gules a lion and a border countercoloured'. In the early rolls countercoloured is described as 'de l'un en l'autre'.

The choice of the devices in a shield seems often to have been quite arbitrary, the chief care being to see that one

Fig. 69.   Cockfield
(*Silver three cocks gules*)

Fig. 70.   Corbet
(*Gold two corbies*)

Fig. 71.   Arundel
(*Silver six swallows*)

Fig. 72.   Grey

man's arms differed in some way from another's; but the selection was often made, where possible, so as to pun upon the bearer's name. Some of these selections are obvious at sight, like the cocks of Cockfield (fig. 69), the swines' heads of Swinford, and the corbies of Corbet (fig. 70). Others depend upon the French nomenclature of the rolls, like the *hirondelles* of Arundel (fig. 71), the *herises* of Harris, and the *pennes* of Coupen. A few are of more recondite nature, such as the barry coat of Grey, which resembles a *gré* or ladder (fig. 72). Any of the rolls of arms, pictorial or written, will furnish further examples (see Chapter VI).

CHAPTER III

DIFFERENCING AND MARSHALLING OF ARMS

ONE noticeable feature in the rolls of arms is the frequent occurrence of shields that are similar, and differ only in their colouring, or the exchange of one charge for another, or by some small addition. This usually indicates either relation-

Fig. 73. Mortimer

Fig. 74. Roger Mortimer
'le oncle'

Fig. 75. John Mortimer
of Herefordshire

Fig. 76. Roger Mortimer
of Herefordshire

ship, or a desire to distinguish between different members of a family, or to show the feudal connexion between one house and another.

Thus in the Great Roll, Roger Mortimer bears the well-known arms of his house (fig. 73), which may be translated literally, 'barry gold and azure with the chief paly and the corners gyronny with a silver scutcheon'. Roger Mortimer 'le oncle' has the same arms with the scutcheon of ermine (fig. 74). John Mortimer of Herefordshire charges the silver scutcheon with a saltire gules (fig. 75), and another Roger, also of Herefordshire, with a purple lion (fig. 76); while Henry Mortimer changes the blue of the original arms to red. Five Staffordshire knights in the same roll, all of the house of Hastang, furnish another interesting group:

Fig. 77. Hastang

Robert, the head of the house, bearing 'azure a chief gules (or party fessewise gules and azure) and a lion gold'; while his son John adds to the same a silver label. Another Robert Hastang bears the lion with a forked tail (fig. 77); Richard Hastang adds to the original arms a silver baston; and Philip Hastang bears the lion silver instead of gold.

Perhaps the most familiar instance of differenced arms is the shield of the Prince of Wales, who bears the royal arms of his father the King with a silver label. The label is of quite early origin, and consists of a narrow stripe crossing the top of the shield with three, four, or five tags, or 'pieces' as they were called, hanging from it (fig. 78). There is no meaning in the number of pieces, nor any rule

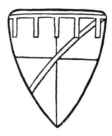

Fig. 78. Early form of label from the shield (*quarterly gules and gold a baston sable and a label silver*) of Henri de Laci earl of Lincoln in Westminster abbey church

as to the colour of labels, and the pieces themselves often carried charges like roundels or castles, or were checkered or of ermine. Another early way of differencing was to enclose the paternal arms with a border, as did Thomas of Woodstock, the youngest of Edward III's sons (fig. 79); and during the fourteenth century some of the bishops differenced their father's arms with an engrailed border, like those of the

Fig. 79. Thomas of Wood-
stock duke of Gloucester
(*Old France and England
quarterly with a silver border*)

Fig. 80. William Bateman
bishop of Norwich (*Sable a
crescent ermine and a border
engrailed silver*)

founder of Trinity Hall in Cambridge (fig. 80). The blue and silver gobony border of the Beauforts is another familiar case of differencing (fig. 81)

A distinction between the arms of a father and his younger sons was often made by adding some small charge, like a

Fig. 81. Beaufort

crescent, star, or martlet, but the difficulty of continuing such a scheme logically has led to its disuse to a very large extent.

It was customary from quite early times for the daughters of a house, whether married or single, to bear their father's arms undifferenced; it was therefore but natural that a man should wish to show his connexion with another house by displaying the arms of his wife with his own. This was done at first by simply setting them side by side, or on other equal terms. But at quite an early date husband and wife some-times showed heraldically that they were one by 'dimidi-ating' or 'halving' the two shields of their arms and then joining together a half of each to make one shield. A good illustration is at hand in the arms above referred to as drawn by Matthew Paris before 1253, which include, amongst others, a shield with a fer-de-moline or millrind halved with

a rampant lion. The well-known arms of the Cinque Ports, first found on the Dover seal of 1305, furnish another early example (fig. 82). Halving arms could however rarely be done without producing odd or inartistic effects, as in the examples just cited, and early in the fourteenth century it was abandoned in favour of a more logical combination.

Fig. 82. The Cinque Ports. (England halved with *azure three gold hulls of ships*)

This consisted in 'impaling' or 'departing' the whole content of the two shields side by side in one, and this way of displaying the arms of man and wife still holds (fig. 83).

It is not easy to say when impaling first came in, but in the inventory of the ornaments in the vestry of Christchurch, Canterbury, taken in 1315–16 a cope given to the church on his consecration and profession by Peter Quivil, bishop of Exeter, in 1280, is described as 'Capa Petri Exoniensis Episcopi cum scutis bipartitibus de Baudekino'.

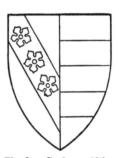

Fig. 83. Cookesey (*Silver a bend azure and three gold cinqfoils pierced on the bend*) impaling Harcourt (*gules two gold bars*), from a brass at Kidderminster

Much about the same time that arms began to be impaled they were quartered together, as in the shields of Castile and Leon on the tomb of Queen Eleanor (fig. 84), or of Old France and England on the tomb of King Edward III, first adopted by him in 1340. The Queen's

23

quartered arms are among the earliest, since they were brought in on her marriage to King Edward I in 1254.

Fig. 84. Quartered shield of Queen Eleanor on her tomb in Westminster abbey church

Another early example is to be found in the Great Roll in the arms of Sir Simon Montagu, which are described as 'quarterly silver and azure in the azure quarters the griffins of gold and in the silver quarters the daunces of gules'.

(Quartile de argent e de azure en les quarters de azure les griffons de or en les quarters de argent les daunces goules.)

Both in Queen Eleanor's case and that of King Edward III the quartered arms represent two kingdoms under one

Fig. 85. Phelip (*Quarterly gules and silver with an eagle of gold in the quarter*)

Fig. 86. Despenser (*Quarterly silver and gules fretty gold with a baston sable*)

Fig. 87. Arms of Hugh Stafford lord Bourchier (1 and 4, *Stafford with a molet sable on the cheveron*; 2 and 3, *silver a cross engrailed gules and four water-skins sable*). From his stall-plate at Windsor

sovereign, but the same principle was extended later to represent a dignity, such as an earldom or barony, to which a man became entitled by descent or marriage, or to show that he was the inheritor of some estate through a wise and

25

prudent marriage on the part of his father. Such quartered arms must not, of course, be confounded with arms like those of the Phelips (fig. 85), or the Says, or the Despensers (fig. 86), whose shields were quarterly from the first.

Fig. 88. Seal of Humphrey Stafford earl of Buckingham, Northampton, Essex, and Perche, as captain of Calais and lieutenant of the Marches, 1442

Good examples of arms quartered for dignities are to be found among the enamelled stall-plates of the Knights of the Garter at Windsor. Thus Sir Hugh Stafford (*ob.* 1420) quarters with his own arms those of his wife Elizabeth, in her own right baroness Bourchier, on which account he was summoned to parliament as lord Bourchier (fig. 87). After his death the lady married another K.G., Sir Lewis Robsart (*ob.* 1431), who also through her became lord Bourchier, and quartered her arms with his own. Another Stafford, Sir Humphrey, who succeeded his father when a child as earl of Stafford, became on the death of his mother (Anne, sister and heir of Humphrey duke of Gloucester) in 1438,

earl of Buckingham, Northampton, Essex, and Perche. His shield on his seal (fig. 88) is accordingly quarterly of (1) Buckingham, (2) Bohun of Hereford and Essex, (3) Bohun of Northampton, and (4) Stafford. In 1424 Richard Nevill, son of Ralph earl of Westmorland and the lady Joan Beaufort, married Alice, daughter of Thomas earl of Salisbury, and became in right of his wife earl of Salisbury, lord Montagu, and lord Monthermer.

Fig. 89. Arms, from his stall-plate, of Richard Nevill earl of Salisbury, lord Montagu, and lord Monthermer

He accordingly quartered with his own arms, which were 'gules a silver saltire and a label of Beaufort', those of Montagu quartering Monthermer (fig. 89). His brother William married about 1426 Joan, daughter and heir of Thomas lord Fauconberg, whom he succeeded in the title, and quartered his arms with his own. One other interesting example in connexion with a dignity is furnished by the stall-plate of Thomas lord Stanley (*ob.* 1458–9), who quarters with his own quartered arms those of the kingdom of Man, of which island he was lord.

The stall-plates also afford instances of arms quartered through succession to estates. Thus Sir William Arundel (*ob.* 1400) quarters with his paternal arms those of his mother, daughter and co-heir of John lord Maltravers (fig. 90), and William lord Willoughby (*ob.* 1409) those of his grandmother, who was daughter and co-heir of Robert Ufford earl of Suffolk (fig. 91). Sir John Grey of Ruthin, as an eldest son, differences with a silver label the arms of his father, Rainald lord Grey of Ruthin, who in 1391 became lord Hastings on the death of his relative John Hastings earl

Fig. 90. Arms of Sir William Arundel, K.G., from his stall-plate

Fig. 91. Arms of William lord Willoughby, K.G., from his stall-plate

of Pembroke, and quartered with his own arms of Grey those of Hastings quartering Valence (fig. 92). A similar example is afforded by the plate of Sir John Astley, who differences with an ermine label the arms of his father Sir Thomas Astley, quartered with those of his mother, daughter and heir of Sir Robert Harcourt (fig. 93).

Another way of marshalling arms by a man who has married an heiress is by superposing the lady's arms in a smaller shield upon the middle of his own shield. Such superposed shield is now called 'a scutcheon of pretence'. A good early example is afforded by the seal of Richard

Beauchamp earl of Warwick, who bears upon his quartered shield of Beauchamp and Newburgh a small quartered shield of Clare and Despenser for his second wife (m. 1423), Isabel,

Fig. 92. Arms of Sir John Grey of Ruthin, K.G., from his stall-plate

Fig. 93. Arms of Sir John Astley, K.G., from his stall-plate

Fig. 94. Arms of Richard Beauchamp earl of Warwick, with a scutcheon of pretence of the arms of Clare and Despenser

daughter of Richard lord Despenser and earl of Gloucester, and widow of Richard earl of Worcester (fig. 94). The seal of John Tiptoft, engraved probably on his creation as earl of Worcester in 1449, gives another instance (fig. 95). It shows the quarters of Tiptoft and Powis (the earl's mother) with a superposed shield of the arms (1, Montagu; 2 and 3, Monthermer; 4, Nevill with a label) of his first wife Cecily, daughter of Richard Nevill earl of Salisbury, and widow of Henry duke of Warwick.

Fig. 95. Seal of John Tiptoft earl of Worcester, 1449

It has ever been lawful for a man to impale his arms with those attaching to any office or dignity he may hold. Bishops, for instance, have impaled their arms with those of their cathedral church or see since at least the end of the fourteenth century, and abbots and priors were wont to do the same as regards the arms of their abbey or priory. Deans of secular churches, heads of colleges, the Regius professors at Cambridge (since 1590), and the kings-of-arms, have also had and have the same privilege. It is not, however, regular for a man to combine with such official arms those of his wife, and if he be a knight of an Order like the Garter, he must not encircle with the Garter or Collar of any Order an impaled shield, but only his own arms. Should a man who is a widower marry again, he may cease to marshal the arms of his first wife; but he may also, should he will, continue to bear them, with those of his second wife, impaled with his own. The same rule holds as to the arms of a twice or more times married lady.

CHAPTER IV

LOZENGES, ROUNDELS, AND BANNERS OF ARMS

I T is the custom to-day for the arms of widows and spinsters to be displayed on a lozenge instead of a shield. This custom does not go much further back than the reign of Elizabeth; and the monument at Westminster of Frances duchess of Suffolk, *ob.* 1559, is an early example. But the use of a lozenge as a variant from the more usual shield of arms is much earlier, and was invented by the seal engravers in the thirteenth century. An example of a lozenge of arms occurs on a seal of Thomas Furnival, who died in 1279, and instances of its use for the arms of men may be found on their seals for at least a century later. Lozenges of arms may be met with almost equally soon on the seals of ladies, an early example being that of Joan countess of Surrey, 1306. But the lozenge was not reserved for the lady's arms, and the seal in question shows five lozenges in cross, that in the middle bearing her husband's checkers, and the others the arms of her father and her mother. Another lady's seal, that of Maud countess of Oxford, 1336, has her husband's shield in the middle, and four lozenges of the arms of her father and herself, of her mother, and of her first husband. Maud of Lancaster in 1344 also shows on her seal the shields of arms of her two husbands side by side with lozenges of Lancaster above for her father and herself, and of Chaworth below for her mother.

About the same time as the lozenge the seal-engravers introduced, for a like reason, roundels of arms. These, too, were used indiscriminately for the arms of men and women in the same way as lozenges. An early instance is afforded by the seal of Mary countess of Pembroke, 1322, which has the halved arms of her husband and herself in a shield (fig. 96) between roundels of the arms of her mother, of King Edward II, and of Queen Isabel.

Both lozenges and roundels of arms were also used decoratively. They are to be found side by side on the embroidered orfrey, of late thirteenth-century work, of the famous Syon cope now in the Victoria and Albert Museum, which has also for its border a contemporary stole and fanon, worked throughout with lozenges of arms (fig. 97). In the same collection is a beautiful enamelled coffer of the same date as the Syon cope, also decorated throughout with armorial lozenges; and similar lozenges of the arms of England and Valence form a diaper on the remains

Fig. 96. Valence dimidiated or halved with Seynt-Pol

of the gilt-latten plate beneath the effigy of William earl of Pembroke (*ob.* 1296) in the abbey church of Westminster. The pillows of the effigies in the same church of Edmund Crouchback and his wife Aveline countess of Lancaster, are also painted with armorial lozenges. A fine and large roundel of brilliant enamel, with a gold charbocle on a field party gules and azure, forms part of the stall-plate of Ralph lord Bassett (*ob.* 1386) (fig. 98).

An early inventory of Christchurch, Canterbury, specifies a large number of vestments worked with shields and lozenges of arms and in one case with arms *in quadrangulis*. These might have been square or oblong like those on the band of the Syon cope, but they are in any case suggestive of the display of heraldry on banners.

Banners of arms were freely used throughout the medieval

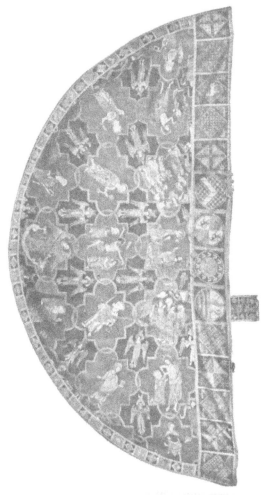

Fig. 97. The Syon cope, now in the Victoria
and Albert Museum

34

period, not only in the field, but in every kind of decoration. Everyone is familiar with the banner of the royal arms (miscalled the royal standard) that betokens the presence of the King, and with our national banner called the Union Jack, which is compounded of the banners of St George,

Fig. 98. Enamelled roundel from the stall-plate of Ralph lord Bassett

St Andrew, and St Patrick (fig. 99). The banner of the arms of the city of London, which is flown constantly over the Mansion House when the lord mayor is in residence, is also familiar to many. Banners of arms were used decoratively as borders to the beautiful figures *temp*. Henry III formerly in the Painted Chamber at Westminster, and a similar use of them may be seen in old painted glass windows of the fourteenth century in York Minster and divers other places. The banners of the Templars and Hospitallers are figured in the MS. by Matthew Paris already referred to, and that of Simon de Montfort, 'party indented of silver and gules', is blazoned in Glover's Roll of Arms (fig. 100). Large banners

Fig. 99. The Union Jack, with the component banners of
St George, St Andrew, and St Patrick

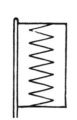

Fig. 100. Banner of
Simon de Montfort

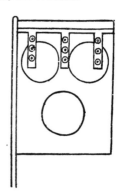

Fig. 101. Banner of the arms of
Sir Peter Courtenay, K.G., from
his stall-plate (the staff added)

of arms upheld by lions and eagles form a conspicuous feature of the tomb of Sir Lewis Robsart at Westminster, and enamelled armorial banners serve as stall-plates for many of the early Knights of the Garter (fig. 101).

In all these cases, and in every other previous to the Tudor period, the banners have the longer sides upright, and this is the only shape that allows the heraldry to be displayed properly upon it. It will be found by a comparison of examples that throughout the fourteenth and fifteenth centuries, when the artistic treatment of heraldry was at its highest level, special care was taken in all the best examples to cover the field of a shield, lozenge, roundel, or banner as far as possible with whatever was placed upon it; and to maintain a proper balance of colour between field and charges, even when the charge was but a simple ordinary, like the bend of the Scropes, or the saltire of the Nevills, or the cross of St George. With an upright banner all this is easy, but when, as is the present practice, most banners are twice as long as they are wide, and flown with their narrower end next the staff, it is often impossible to draw properly such charges as the English leopards, the Scottish lion, or the Irish harp upon the Sovereign's banner, in which as usually drawn the charges are compressed vertically and stretched horizontally, yet there is still space 'to let' at the side. The difference may readily be seen in the banners of the Queen Mother or Queen Mary, each of which contains the Arms of the Sovereign in a square impaling a second square with the Consort's own arms. This banner is of course twice as long as it need be, but its greater richness of effect when compared with the Queen's banner is quite noteworthy. The field of a banner was almost always used for the display of arms only, which of course covered it; but in several of the banner stall-plates the Knight's shield with its crested helm

37

and flowing mantling is displayed upon the field, and this in the fifteenth century. Banners were not unfrequently fringed, sometimes with gold, sometimes with a fringe of two or more colours.

A standard differed entirely from a banner both in shape and contents. It was a long and narrow flag, with the lower edge horizontal, and the upper aslant from the staff to the

Fig. 102. Shield of St Edward with rounded corners, in Westminster abbey church

end, which was slit for a little way. An upright panel next the staff always contained the arms of St George, and the rest of the field was parted fessewise, or into three or four bars, and powdered with badges. It was also divided into three parts by two bends with the owner's word, reason, or motto, and the first section then contained the crest or principal badge. The whole was fringed of the livery colours. Standards varied in size with the dignity of the owner, that of the King being twice as long as a knight's, while those of peers were of intermediate length according to their rank.

Standards were only used for parade purposes and funerals, and were finally hung above the owner's grave.

It has been pointed out that the shape of a shield is quite immaterial and of no heraldic significance, but it may not be without interest to examine some of its forms. The earliest

Fig. 103. Shield on a brass at Stoke Poges, Bucks., 1476

shields were long and kite-shaped, the better to protect the holder, and a survival of this appears in the rounded corners of the early shields behind the quire of Westminster abbey church (see figs. 3 and 102), and in many early seals. Then the shield became shorter, and its corners were made square, and this heater-shaped form has continued in use down to to-day. During the fourteenth century shields often had a tendency to become more straight-sided and almost rounded at the bottom, to afford more room for the charges and devices carved and painted upon them. In the fifteenth

century there came into fashion for decorative purposes
shields of similar form to the notched and curved ones used
in the lists, and sometimes the field was worked into a series
of vertical grooves. An unusually ornate shield is shown in

Fig. 104. Diapered shield *c.* 1345, in Beverley Minster

fig. 103. Numerous varieties of this form were popular in
the Tudor period, and quite naturally adapted themselves
to the influences of the Renaissance. Beautiful examples
are to be seen at Cambridge in King's College Chapel and
on the gatehouses of Christ's and St John's Colleges; and of

English work in gilt-bronze upon the tomb of Henry VII and his Queen, and that of the lady Margaret, his mother, at Westminster.

A charming feature to be found at all dates in pictorial heraldry is the relieving of the plain surfaces of both fields and ordinaries on shields and banners of arms with the delicate decoration called diapering. Examples may be seen on all sides, on seals, and on monuments, and especially in heraldic glass. Some of the finest examples in carved work are the diapered shields on the monument of the lady Eleanor Percy in Beverley Minster (fig. 104).

CHAPTER V

CRESTS, BADGES, REBUSES AND SUPPORTERS

ALMOST as early as the introduction of armorial shields there came into being the objects known as crests. A crest, as its name implies, was originally a feathered plume on the head of a bird. Such a plume or bush of feathers, as it was called, was fixed as an ornament in the top of a helm, and thus formed the crest of its wearer. As early as 1198, on his second great seal, King Richard I has upon his cylindrical helm two wing-shaped fans turned in opposite directions, with a leopard below upon the cap; and similar fan-shaped bushes were popular throughout the thirteenth century. Other devices came into use later, and in time became associated with individuals; and eventually, like arms, they were looked upon as hereditary. Roger of Leybourne, before his death in 1284, used a lion for a crest, and before 1300 Thomas earl of Lancaster and his brother Henry both used seals whereon their helms are surmounted by wivers or two-legged dragons. The like creature also crests the earl's horse's head. The crest was at first fixed alone and directly upon the helm, but early in the fourteenth century it was often encircled by a crown (figs. 105, 106, and 108), or placed upon the hat or cap of estate that was sometimes worn over the helm. The funeral crest of Edward Prince of Wales above his tomb at Canterbury is a good example of this form. The crest was always something that could be worn, and if it represented an object that was naturally too large or too heavy, a model of it was made in boiled leather, like the Prince's leopard at Canterbury, or of wood or other light material. Such crests as the pictorial scenes and other absurdities granted to generals and admirals during the eighteenth and nineteenth centuries could hardly have been conceived while heraldry was a living art.

Fig. 105. Crested helm upon the tomb of Richard Beauchamp earl of Warwick

The helm of which the crest formed part was such an one as was included in the war harness of the time, and it was usually drawn in profile the better to display the crest, which of course faced the same way as its wearer. Front-facing helms and crests likewise occur, both on seals and monuments, but the modern custom of using helms of different types facing different ways to denote grades of rank has no ancient precedent, and is impossible to defend logically.

43

The crown that so often encircles crests is purely an ornamental adjunct (figs. 106 and 108), and as devoid of meaning as the cap of estate, notwithstanding that in the fourteenth and fifteenth centuries this formed part of the insignia at the investiture of a duke. The crowns generally consisted of three, four, or five fleurons or ornate leaves set upon a jewelled circlet, and were not necessarily always of gold or silver. In that great storehouse of coloured medieval

Fig. 106. Seal of Walter lord Hungerford with crest and flanking banners of arms, *c.* 1420

armory, the stall-plates of the Knights of the Garter, two of the early plates have the crowns enamelled blue, and quite a number of others have red crowns; and there is no reason for regarding these as exceptional.

The cap of estate appears first, with his leopard crest, upon the head of the armed and mounted figure of King Edward III (apparently for his dignity as duke of Normandy and Aquitaine) on the new great seal made for him after the Peace of Bretigny in 1339–40. After 1350 it came into common use as a base for crests, and was so employed not only by dukes who had been invested with it, but by earls and barons, and even by knights, who certainly had not (fig. 107). The cap of estate was generally red, with the

Fig. 107. Seal of Edmund Beaufort duke of Somerset, *c.* 1445, with leopard crest on a cap of estate

brim turned up with ermine; but in two of the stall-plates the cap is blue.

Whether the crested helm were encircled by a crown or surmounted by the cap of estate, it was often covered behind with a hanging scarf or cloth, sometimes with tasseled ends. In the latter part of the fourteenth century, when this mantling, as it is called, first became fashionable, it was of quite simple character. But it soon developed pictorially into something larger and more ornamental until it extended

45

on both sides of the helm in a series of graceful twists flung about with charming freedom. The usual colour of the mantling, like that of the cap of estate with which it was often associated, was red with a lining of ermine or minever, but there was no rigid rule as to this before the seventeenth century. Thus, out of the sixty earliest stall-plates at Windsor,

Fig. 108. Feathered mantling from the stall-plate, *c.* 1422–3, of Sir Hugh Courtenay, K.G.

only about one-third have a plain red mantling. Seven are black, six white, two blue (in each case with a powdering of gold fleurs-de-lis), and one green with gold spots; two are all ermine, and another is all of gold. Six are covered with silver feathers, because the crest (such as a swan's head) suggested it (fig. 108), and quite a number are of two different colours, such as black and white, red and black, white and blue, on either side of the helm. One is quarterly fessewise indented of red and white, another paly of red and white, and a third of ermine with red bars; while others have the outside powdered with gold lozenges or trefoils, or gold branches and flowers. Two brothers of the Bourchier family powder their red mantlings with gold billets, and the white lining with bouces and Bourchier knots; and a Lovel knight has a purple mantling powdered with gold hanging-locks (fig. 109).

Towards the end of the fourteenth century the junction of the crest with the helm began to be masked, in the same way as with the earlier crowns, by a twisted wreath or torse

Fig. 109. Crested helm, and mantling powdered with his badge, of Francis lord Lovel, K.G., c. 1483, from his stall-plate

of two or more differently coloured stuffs (fig. 109). This is now usually described as 'a wreath of the colours', that is to say, the principal colour and metal of the arms, but the medieval artist held himself as free in the matter as in the colour of the mantlings. Nor did he confine himself to the six twists of modern rule, but showed a lesser or greater number as he pleased.

The decadence of heraldry which began under the Tudor kings is responsible for detaching the torse and crest and representing them apart from the helm to which they belong, and modern ignorance has perverted the torse into

47

a twisted bar. In this form people are content to display what they call their 'crest' upon their spoons and forks, the panels of carriages and cars, or the buttons of liveried servants. Were the torse omitted the crest would logically become and could be used as a badge.

Fig. 110. The falcon and fetterlock badge of the house of York. From King Henry VII's chapel at Westminster

A badge is any device or figure assumed as a distinctive mark or emblem by an individual or family, and should be borne alone, without any shield, torse, or other accessory. But whereas a crest is distinctly personal to its owner, his badge may be worn by whom he pleases, and so would properly supersede the incorrect 'crest' upon the livery buttons of men-servants. Badges were anciently used as ornaments or decorations in every conceivable way, and were often accompanied by an appropriate word, reason, or motto. There was as great variety in the choice of badges as in that of crests. Not infrequently the same device served both for crest and badge; but as a rule it was different. Examples of badges abound. The bear and ragged staff of the Beauchamps, the crescent of the Percys, the swan of the

Figs. 111, 112. Badges of King Henry VII in the chapel of King's College, Cambridge

Bohuns, the mermaid of the Berkeleys, the sickles of the Hungerfords, the knots of the Staffords and Bourchiers, the molet of the Veres, the red rose of the Lancastrians, the falcon and fetterlock (fig. 110) and white rose of the house of York, the Beaufort portcullis and the Tudor rose (figs. 111, 112), and the ostrich feathers borne by the sons of Queen Philippa and their descendants, are all familiar instances. Many men had more than one badge. Thus bishop Peter Courtenay's famous chimney-piece in the palace at Exeter displays dolphins, swans and boars, St Anthony's tau-cross and bell, and the sickles and sheaves of the Hungerfords with whom he was connected. And John de Vere, the thirteenth earl of Oxford, bore, besides the molet from his arms and the harpy which did duty as one of his supporters, a cranket or jack and a boar (*verre*) in allusion to his name, an ox crossing a ford in token of his title, a gold whistle for his office of lord high admiral, and a chair of estate for his hereditary office of lord great chamberlain.

Such allusive devices as the Vere boar of the earl of Oxford form what is called a rebus, or word punning upon a man's name. Rebuses were very popular all through the fifteenth and sixteenth centuries, and are to be met with even in the thirteenth and fourteenth. Thus long swords are to be found on Longespee seals in the thirteenth century, and a boar occurs on the seal of Hugh de Veer appended to the Barons' letter of 1300–1. Aver of Rochford used in 1333 a seal with sheaves of oats flanking his shield as a pun on his Christian name, and Thomas duke of Gloucester, son of Edward III, because he was born at Woodstock, used the stock of a dead tree. Richard lord Grey of Codnor (*ob.* 1418) has on his seal a 'gray' or badger; William lord Botreaux (*ob.* 1461) has buttresses; Thomas lord Ros of Hamlake or Hemsley (*ob.* 1464), hemlocks; and the lady Margaret Beaufort, *marguerites*.

Many bishops, abbots, and priors marked with their rebuses parts of buildings erected by them. In the cathedral church of Norwich bishop Walter Lyhart used a *hart ly*ing in *water*, and bishop Goldwell *gold*en *well*s; at Wells bishop Beckington used a *beacon* on a *tun*; and at Ely bishop Alcock has a *cock* on the globe as being *all* the world. At Canterbury cardinal John Morton has an eagle on a *tun* which probably was lettered 'mor'; prior Oxney an *ox* with *ne* upon him;

Fig. 113. Rebus of John Islip abbot of Westminster

Fig. 114. **Seal** of William lord Hastings, 1461,
with supporters

4-2

and prior Goldstone II, *gold stone*s. At Exeter bishop Old-
ham has an *owl* with a scroll lettered 'dom'; at Westminster
(fig. 113) abbot Islip has an *eye* and a *slip* of a fig tree, with
a man falling ('I slip!'), and at Fountains abbot Darnton
has 'dern' on a *tun*, and abbot Huby a *hobby* or small hawk.

Fig. 115. Seal of John Nevill lord Montagu (*ob.* 1471)
showing use of supporters

Quite soon after the engravers began to design armorial
seals they felt the want of something to fill up the space
between a shield of arms and the circle in which it was set.
First they introduced scrollwork, then a wiver or other
creature, next a secondary shield, or perhaps a badge. Two
lions back to back with intertwined tails also did service.
Then such beasts were turned round to grasp the shield, and
so became supporters. The growing popularity of crests soon
caused the crested helm to be placed above the shield, and

then the engraver skilfully transferred to the supporters of a shield the duty of upholding the heavy helm instead. The resulting compositions are usually drawn with consummate grace and skill, and the seals of the middle of the fifteenth century which were the first to complete the evolution of such designs are among the finest of these beautiful works of art (see figs. 4, 88, 95, 107, and 114 and 115). The use of supporters is now restricted to peers, Knights of the Garter and of some other Orders, and a few privileged baronets and commoners, but ancient heraldic freedom allowed supporters to a knight as well as an earl or duke.

CHAPTER VI

ROLLS OF ARMS, AND HERALDRY OF THE THIRTEENTH & FOURTEENTH CENTURIES

An analysis of the early rolls of arms, both pictorial and descriptive, illustrates very clearly the simplicity which is so characteristic of all English heraldry down to the sixteenth century. Many rolls date from a few years before or not long after 1300; but as the principle of hereditary arms was by then fully established, the heraldry of the fourteenth and fifteenth centuries is largely that of the preceding period, with one or two innovations which will be noted in their place.

One of the earliest of the written rolls is that in the Heralds' College (MS. L. 14), known as Glover's. It dates from about 1255, and out of a total of some two hundred and fifty shields as many as eighty are formed by simple combinations of the ordinaries; another thirty consist of ordinaries with charges on or about them; and twenty others are simply quarterly, checky, vairy, bendy, barry, gyronny, or masculy. Of the remainder, twenty-six have lions or leopards, one an ox, and two have eagles. The ox (*ung kene*) is appropriately borne by Rowland de Okstede, as are three boars' heads by Adam de Swyneburne. So, too, Thomas Corbet has two black *corbeaux* or corbies, Odinel Heron three herons, and Geoffry de Lucy three luces or pike (fig. 116). Nicholas de Moeles bears 'two bars with three molets in the chief', and Roger de Merley 'barry of silver and gules with a border of azure and gold merlots in the border'. 'Merlots' or martlets occur in several other arms; also 'papegayes' or popinjays and black cocks. Rauf de Gorges quite properly has a whirlpool

(Lat. *gurges*), described as 'roele dargent et dazur', and William Montagu three *montes acuti*, which are blazoned or described as 'ung fesse engrele de trois pieces' (fig. 117). A ray of the sun is the sole charge of one shield, and another has a crescent in a border of martlets. Other charges oc-

Fig. 116. Lucy (*gules three luces breathing gold*)

Fig. 117. Montagu

Fig. 118. Gacelyn (*gold sown with billets sable*)

Fig. 119. Zouche (*gules sown with gold besants*)

curring in the roll are roses, sheaves, scutcheons, scallops, fleurs-de-lis, maunches or sleeves, bouces or water-skins, crosslets, stars, breys or hempbreakers, cinqfoils and sexfoils, horseshoes (*des fers*), and pillows (*horielers*). Roundels of silver or gules called 'torteux' or 'torteaulx' and of gold called besants likewise occur.

In six cases the field is simply fretty, in one strewn with billets (fig. 118), and in another sown with besants (fig. 119).

Besides five shields with ordinary crosses (in one case between charges, in another with charges upon it) there are five others with crosses paty, '*patonce*', or 'floretee', forked crosses, and a 'false cross', that is, a cross with the middle part cut away to show the field. In a similar way an orle is

called a 'false scutcheon', and six flat rings are 'faux rondelettes' (fig. 120). In one case a shield with six 'mascles' has them 'voided of the field' (fig. 122).

The so-called Roll of Caerlaverock, to which reference is often made, is not properly speaking a roll at all, but a poem giving an account of the siege of Caerlaverock castle in 1300, with descriptions in French of about one hundred arms and banners of the earls, barons, and knights who were there. The terms used are similar to those of the Great Roll.

Fig. 120. John de Vipount (*gules six false-roundels gold*)

The Great Roll, as it may be called for convenience, was compiled by some unknown hand and for some unknown but apparently special reason, between 1308 and 1314, and contains the blazons or descriptions of the arms of more than eleven hundred persons, arranged for the most part under the counties in which they held their lands. It is therefore a document of the highest importance, not only from its length, but because it probably determined for a long time forward the plain and simple language of medieval heraldry, a subject to which further reference will be made later. It also includes the arms of a large number of those who fought at Caerlaverock, and of the signatories to the famous Barons' Letter of 1300–1, whose armorial seals can thus profitably be compared with the blazons of the roll.

The contents of the Great Roll are of similar character to those of Glover's Roll, and include, like it, a large number of arms based simply upon combinations of the ordinaries.

There is still confusion between engrailed and indented: the former term being usually restricted to crossses, saltires, bends, and bastons; the latter to chiefs, fesses, and borders. But many 'indented' borders are known to have been really engrailed. The matter does not become clearer when the 'cross engrele' of Eustace de la Hache is found to be engrailed (fig. 39) on his seal, but indented on his counter-seal (fig. 121); or when William le Marechal's 'bende engrele' appears plainly on his seal as indented of five pieces; or when

Fig. 121. *Gold a cross indented or engrailed gules.* Eustace de la Hache

Fig. 122. *Gules seven gold lozenges voided.* The earl of Winchester

the Caerlaverock poem describes Elys Daubeny's 'fesse endente' as engrailed. Engrailing and indenting were therefore the same thing, though not always drawn in the same way. It is interesting to note that engrailing is not yet extended to a cheveron. Another point worthy of notice is that in this and other early rolls lozenges and mascles are exactly the opposite of the same charges to-day. Thus the arms of the earl of Winchester are blazoned as 'de gules a vij losenges de or', which contemporary seals show to be what are now called 'mascles' and Glover's Roll blazons the same arms as 'mascles voydes de champ' (fig. 122). The earl of Kent, on the other hand, has 'mascle de ver e de gules', or what is now 'lozengy vair and gules'.

As might be expected from its greater length, the roll under notice brings in many more kinds of charges than Glover's

Roll. These include wivers, griffins, bears and leverers; heads of boars, beasts (*testes-de-bis*), wolves, stags, and of cats; cocks, eagles, corbies, herons, 'merelots', popinjays, falcons and 'girfauks', as well as silver feathers and eagles' wings. Dolphins, luces, herrings, scallops, and shields with barry or wavy fields, represent the waters; and trefoils, sheaves of wheat and barley, burdock and mulberry leaves, an oak tree and chaplets, the products of the earth, as well as the roses, cinqfoils and fleurs-de-lis before noticed; while a sun's ray, crescents, and molets or stars come from the skies. Manu-

Fig. 123. *Gold a lion rampant purpure.* The earl of Lincoln

Fig. 124. *Gold a leaping lion gules.* Roger Felbrigg

factured articles comprise bernaks or breys, besants of gold and silver, bouces, bosons or birdbolts, the staves called bourdons, buckles, cups of silver, cushions, gloves, hammers, horseshoes, pitchers, rings, and roundels pierced and plain, rowels or pierced molets, a lady's sleeve (in several cases with her hand also), chess-rooks, trumpets, vans or winnowing baskets, and Danish axes. Castles and a battled fesse are the only reminders of building. Lions or lions rampant (fig. 123) are very popular, and are often adorned with crowns and collars; they likewise appear with forked tails. Three or more lions are called lioncels. Lions passant or walking also occur, and a single case of a leaping lion (fig. 124). Leopards, or lions that look at one, are always walking, and sometimes crowned (fig. 125). Lions are gold, silver, and of all colours, as well as of ermine and vair, or powdered with drops and billets. They also occur with barry and fretty coats, and as demi-lions only.

At least fifty of the shields blazoned in the Great Roll belong to the punning class called canting or allusive arms. A few of these appear also in Glover's Roll. The majority are evident enough, such as the 'eschalops' of Eschales, the herrings of Herringaud, the cocks of Cockfield, the trumps of Trumpington, the falcons of John le Fauconer (fig. 126), the bourdons or staves of Bourdon, the boars' heads of the

Fig. 125. *Gules a leopard silver with a crown of gold.* Warren del Yle

Fig. 126. *Silver three falcons gules.* John le Fauconer

Swynefords and Swyneburnes, the roses of Rossell, the barnacks or bernacles of William Bernak, the axes of Hakelut, the wheat-sheaves of Schefeld, and the 'leverers' or greyhounds of Mauleverer. So Adam Martel bears martels or hammers; Adam Videlou and John de Lou, wolves' heads or *testes de lou*; Richard de Catesburi, *testes de cheures* or cats' heads; and Richard de Barlingham a triplet of bears (*ours*). Rauf Cheyndut has a *cheyne* or oak tree, and Guy de Ferre a *fer-de-moline*. A lion with a *pinzon* or chaffinch on the shoulder is borne by Giles Mountpynzon, and two bars and a quarter with a castle in the quarter by William del Chastel. Hugh de Morieus has three *foiles de moures* or mulberry leaves; two of the Wauncy family *gaunz* or gloves; while John and Giles de Argentin and William le Boteler appropriately display silver cups. Piers Bosoun and Thomas de Boltesham bear bosouns or bird-bolts, while Rauf de Zefoul has a cross with a fowl (*oysel*) 'en le cauntel'. This last term occurs several times in both Glover's and the Great Roll, and refers to a charge set in a corner, like that above a bend, with which it is generally associated.

But few varieties of the cross are specified in the Great Roll. The plain cross throughout, or 'crois passant' as it is called in several early rolls, is the most common, and it is also found engrailed. The cross paty, with ends like paws (*pattes*), splayed and split into three divisions, also occurs, as well as the cross with the ends flowered (*les chefs fleurettes*) or sprouting with fleurs-de-lis. The 'crois recercelee' which occurs once, and a second time voided, is clearly a variety of the 'fer-de-moline' or millrind (which occurs seven times in the Great Roll) with its forked extremities curled outwards. Small crosses paty of a flat ended type, or the crosses later called crosslets, were used for the 'crusily' or cross-powdered fields of many shields in the roll.

Reference has already been made to the 'differencing' of arms in order to distinguish those of near relations, like father and son, or to connote feudal connexions. A number of instructive examples are afforded by the Great Roll.

Elder or eldest sons seem usually to have differenced their paternal arms with a label azure, but when the field or the principal charges were already blue, then with a label of silver or of some other colour. Labels of gold, silver, vert, gules, barry, checky, gobony, 'of Pembroke', 'of Valence', etc. also occur in the roll. Arms are likewise frequently differenced, apparently by other than the eldest sons of a house, with an azure or other coloured baston, with a border indented, with a bend, and more rarely with a quarter, a cheveron, or a field powdered with crosses.

The whole question of differencing as regards the Great Roll is however in a fluid state, and there occur such cases as a son merely piercing the molets on his father's bend, or adding a molet to a quarter, or indenting the father's plain border. One nephew adds a bend ermine to the family arms borne by his uncle, and another exchanges his uncle's blue label for a gold one. Three brothers Mauley difference the arms of their house, 'gold a bend sable', by respectively adding on the bend three eagles, three dolphins, and three wivers, all of silver.

Fig. 127. Henry of Lancaster (*England with a baston azure*)

Hugh de Plecy bears 'silver six rowels gules' which John de Plecy differences with a label azure, and his son with an azure baston. Several arms suggest that just as a blue label was the mark of the eldest son, so a blue baston may have denoted a grandson. Thomas earl of Lancaster, for example, bears the arms of his father, England with a label of France; but the arms of his brother Henry of Lancaster were England with a baston azure, which he perhaps bore as a grandson of King Henry III (fig. 127).

The Great Roll also contains a large number of arms of kinsmen of various degrees differenced by such methods as reversal of tinctures, change of ordinary, alteration or modification of charges, etc. Like the arms of sons, these can hardly be claimed as following any definite rule, and it is often very difficult to trace the exact relationship of the bearers.

Bastardy does not seem to have been specially marked so early, and a solitary instance in the roll, of the arms of 'Sire Johan Lovel le bastard', merely adds to the paternal 'wavy of gold and gules' a label of azure with molets of silver.

CHAPTER VII

HERALDRY OF THE FIFTEENTH CENTURY

THE heraldry of the fifteenth century continued, until the incorporation of the heralds in 1484, much on the same lines as those of the fourteenth century, but, as might be expected, with a few additional features of its own. These and the heraldic usage of the century in general are well illustrated by a pictured book of arms about 1460, in the British Museum, in which many of the shields are also accompanied by more or less complete blazons in English.

For example, the arms of the 'Erle of Warreyne' are 'gold and asewre checche'; those of Valence 'sylvyr and asewre berle vij or ix merlettys gowlys'; and the arms of 'Mayster Bowet Byschop of Yorke' (1407–23) 'sylver iij rayndere hedys all of sabyll'.

This interesting collection contains two examples of the curious sub-ordinary called flanches, formed of a pair of curved flanks or segments intruded from the sides of the shield. Thus John Greyby bears an ermine field with two 'flaunchys azure with vi whetherys (wheatears) of golde' (fig. 128); and John Olney 'gowlys besaunte ij flaunches of sabyll (with) ij leberdys sylwyr crownyd w^t gowlys armyd wt asewre'.

Another new feature illlustrated in this collection is the division of the shield into six or nine panes or pieces (Fr. *pointes*). Thus an anonymous shield at the beginning is 'six pieces [gold?] and gules with three pineapples of gold in the gules', and another contains the contemporary example granted in 1456 by John Smert, Garter, to the Tallow-chandlers' Company, and described by him as 'un escu de six points dasur et dargent a trois Coulombes de mesmes membrez de gules portans chacun en son bec ung ramceau dolive dor' (fig. 129). The Girdlers' Company also had a grant in 1454 of 'six pieces of azure and gold with three gold gridirons in the azure'. Thomas Newton 'a beryth goulys and wert ix pecys iiij lebardis headys of gold' (fig. 130), and John Garther 'beryth of ix pecys ermyñ and ermyne'.

Fig. 128. Greyby

Fig. 129. Tallow-
chandlers' Company

Fig. 130. Thomas
Newton

Fig. 131. The Bastard
of Clarence

Another usage of frequent occurrence is that of arms with fields party cheveronwise, but described as 'enty'. Thus 'the bastard of Clarence' (John, son of Thomas duke of Clarence) 'a beryth ente asewre a chef of gowles' with two gold leopards in the chief and a gold fleur-de-lis in the foot (fig. 131); and Sir Bryan Sandford has 'ermyne and sabyll entte' with two boars' heads of gold in the chief; while a third example, the arms of Sir John Goddarde, is blazoned as 'a poynt of sabyll a chefe of goules entte grele (engrailed) iij eglys hedis of sylvyr the bekis gold'.

'Enty' seems actually to be a deep chief of one indenture, like the *pointe* of the French heralds; and in one instance, where it is reversed, the arms of Thorpe are described as the field gold a chefe of asewre entte pycche' with a walking griffin silver, and drawn with two lines issuing from the corners of the shield.

'Enbelyfe' is another rare term, found here (but also much earlier) meaning oblique or bendwise. Thus the arms of Rote are 'sylvyr and sabyll' with a lion 'contyrcolorys enbelyfe after the felde' (fig. 132), and another shield is azure and silver

Fig. 132. Rote   Fig. 133. The Carpenters' Company

an eagle 'enbelyf contyrcolorys armyd with gold'. In the case of a lion the division is usually party bendwise-sinister.

Engrailed cheverons also appear in this collection, and are fortified by the grant in 1466 by William Hawkeslowe, Clarenceux, to the Fellowship of the Craft of Carpenters of 'a felde Silver a Cheveron sable grayled iij Compas of the same' (fig. 133).

Quartered shields appear frequently, as might be expected from the fact that the system of quartering was now fully established.

One curious feature in the drawings in the manuscript is that a pair of beasts or a couple of heads occurring together, as in a chief, are shown facing one another, instead of looking in the same direction, as was more usual.

CHAPTER VIII

GRANTS OF ARMS

THE heraldry of the fifteenth century is further illustrated, both in kind and language, by the documents known as grants of arms.

The origin of grants of arms is somewhat obscure. One obviously spurious example claims to be as early as 1306, and several other grants purport to date from the reign of Edward III. An undoubted grant by King Richard II to Otho de Maundell in 1393 confirms to him the arms, 'gules three gold leopards with silver crowns about their necks', stated to have been granted to his father, Peter de Maundell, by letters patent of King Edward III. In 1389 King Richard also granted arms, 'silver a cap azure with an ostrich feather gules', to John de Kyngeston, and by a patent of 1393–4 authorized Thomas Mowbray, the earl marshal, to exchange the white label about the neck of his gold leopard crest for a silver crown upon its head.

Quite a number of early grants emanate from private individuals, and empower some kinsman or friend and his heirs to bear arms which the grantor is able to transfer to him. Thus Camden prints a grant of 1348–9 from Robert de Morley, marshal of Ireland, to Robert de Corby, of certain arms that had descended to him by the death of Baldwin de Manoures. A more probable grant is one of 1392, whereby Thomas Grendale grants the arms of his cousin and heir, John Beaumeys, which had descended to him, to William Moigne, knight. Another that may be quoted is a charter of Humphrey earl of Stafford and of Perche, dated 13 August 1442, granting to Robert Whitgreve these arms 'azure a quatre points dor quatre cheverons de gules'; and for a crest, a helm with a blue mantling furred with ermine, and a crown and a demi-antelope all of gold. These arms it will be seen may correctly be blazoned as 'nine pieces azure and of Stafford', and it is interesting to notice that in the collection of fifteenth-century arms just described one Richard Whitgreve of Staffordshire, probably a brother or near kinsman of Robert, 'beryth Stafford and sylvyr ix pecys' (fig. 134).

Fig. 134. Whitgreve

Fig. 135. King's College, Cambridge

By letters patent of 14 January 1448–9, King Henry VI granted arms (fig. 135) to his foundation of King's College at Cambridge in unusually florid terms, which may thus be translated from the Latin of the original:

In a black field three silver roses, having in mind that our newly founded college enduring for ages to come, whose perpetuity we wish to be signified by the stability of the black colour, may bring forth the rightest flowers redolent in every kind of sciences: to which also, that we might impart something of regal nobility which might declare the work truly regal and famous, we have ordained to be placed in the chief of the shield parcels of the arms lawfully due to us in our Kingdom of England and France, party of azure with a flower of the French and of gules with a gold leopard passant.

Similar letters patent were issued the same day granting arms to the King's foundation of Eton College in like terms, but substituting 'three lily flowers silver' for the three roses in the King's College arms (fig. 136). King Henry also granted on 30 January 1448–9, to his beloved clerk Nicholas Cloos, for his services in connexion with the building of King's College, these arms: 'silver a cheveron sable with three closed lily-flowers on the cheveron and on a chief sable three silver roses' (fig. 137); and on 19 May 1449, to Roger Keys, clerk, for similar services as regards Eton College, 'party cheveronwise gules and sable three gold keys'

| Fig. 136. | Fig. 137. | Fig. 138. Roger and |
| Eton College | Nicholas Cloos | Thomas Keys |

(fig. 138). This grant was also extended to Thomas Keys, brother of Roger, and his descendants.

The King's and Eton grants, which are still in the possession of the colleges to which they were issued, take the usual form of letters patent, with the great seal appended in green wax, and the shields of arms painted in the middle. The Cloos and Keys grants were no doubt similar, but the arms are only described as *hic depicta*, and not blazoned as in the college grants.

Several other grants of King Henry VI are entered, with the above, on the Close Rolls of his reign, in each case with a drawing of the arms. These are blazoned in only one case, that of the arms granted on 11 March 1444–5 to Bernard Angevin, one of the King's counsellors in Aquitaine: 'Quorum quidem armorum campus est de asura cum uno leone ungulato et linguato de goules ac cum decem floribus per circuitum vocatis *Angevins* de argento.'

The only other known early grant under the great seal is that by King Edward IV in 1472 to Louis de Bruges, seigneur de la Gruthuyse, who had been created earl of Winchester for his kindness to Edward when in exile. This grant is now in the British Museum, and has in the middle an illumination of the arms, which are described as 'dasur a dix Mascles dor enorme dung Canton de nostre propre armes Dangle-terre, Cestassavoir de goulez a ung lipard passaunt dor armee dasur' (that is, 'azure ten gold mascles with a canton of our own arms of England, that is to say of gules with a leopard passant of gold armed azure'). These arms are based upon the old arms of the earldom of Winchester, which are blazoned in the Great Roll as 'de gowles a vij losenges de or'.

One of the earliest grants by a king-of-arms is that to one of the London livery companies, the Drapers', by Sir William Brugges, Garter, in 1439. The original grant, still in the Company's possession, has the blazon 'troys royes de soleil issantz hors de troys nues de flambes coronnez de troys corones imperiales dore [assiser sus une escue dazure]'.

These arms must be a misdescription of the original arms assumed by the Company, which were apparently three pyx-canopies, in the form of lawn or linen veils (such as drapers sold), hanging from beneath triple crowns; this being the usual English fashion.

Of nearly the same date as the above there are recorded a number of grants or confirmations of arms by heralds or kings-of-arms to individuals, but by what authority there is nothing to show.

After the middle of the fifteenth century such grants, whether to London livery companies or individuals, became more common, but the heraldry, as a rule, is of good character, and of similar restrained simplicity to what had hitherto prevailed.

These early grants differ in appearance from the royal letters patent in having the arms depicted in the left-hand margin, and being sealed with the seal of the herald or king-of-arms issuing them.

In connexion with these royal, private, and official grants it is interesting to read the opinion of Nicholas Upton as translated in the famous Book of St Albans, first printed there in 1486. After reciting the several derivations of arms from (1) a father, mother, or other predecessor, or (2) by acquisition through merit, as in the arms of France by King Edward III, or (3) by grant from a prince or 'of sum other lordys', the writer says:

The faurith maner of whise we have thoos armys the wich we take on owre owne propur auctorite. as in theys days opynly we se. how many poore men by thayr grace favoure laboure or deservyng: ar made nobuls...and of theys men mony by theyr awne autorite have take armys to be borne to theym and to ther hayris of whoom it nedys not here to reherse yᵉ namys. Never the lees armys that be so takyn they may lefully and frely beer. Bot yit they be not of so grete dignyte and autorite as thoos armys the wich ar grauntyt day by day by the autorite of a prynce or of a lorde. Yet armys bi a mannys propur auctorite take: if an other man have not borne theym afore: be of strength enogh.

❡ And it is the opynyon of moni men that an herrod of armis may gyve arms. Bot I say if any sych armys be borne by any herrod gyvyn that thoos armys be of no more auctorite then thoos armys the wich be take by a mannys awne auctorite.

CHAPTER IX

HERALDRY IN THE SIXTEENTH CENTURY

IN the first half of the sixteenth century the exuberant treatment of heraldry in art reached its highest point, as may be seen in such buildings as King's College chapel and the gatehouses and other parts of Christ's and St John's Colleges at Cambridge, St George's chapel in Windsor Castle, at Hampton Court, and in Henry VII's chapel at Westminster.

Simultaneously with this gorgeous architectural heraldry there was in certain quarters an outbreak of elaborate arms, in which not only such ordinaries as cheverons and crosses were placed between charges and charged themselves, but a chief with further charges was often added to the shield so as to fill it up as much as possible. The following may serve as illustrations of these crowded compositions:

Thomas Ruthall, bishop of Durham, 1509–23:

Party azure and gules with a cross engrailed and four ring-doves gold and a chief quarterly gold and ermine with two red roses.

Thomas Wulcy, archbishop· of York, 1514–30, and cardinal:

Sable a cross engrailed silver with four leopards' heads azure and a lion passant gules on the cross and a chief gold with a red rose and two choughs.

William Atwater, bishop of Lincoln, 1514–21:

Barry wavy of six pieces ermine and gules with a cheveron and three crayfish gold and a red rose and two gilly flowers on the cheveron. (Granted in 1509.)

John Stokesley, bishop of London, 1530–9:

Lozengy ermine and ermines a cheveron silver with a demi-lion gules and two gillyflowers on the cheveron and a chief azure with a rose between a lily and a pelican, all of gold.

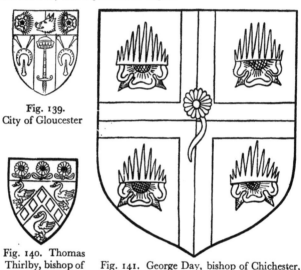

Fig. 139.
City of Gloucester

Fig. 140. Thomas
Thirlby, bishop of
Westminster

Fig. 141. George Day, bishop of Chichester,
from his tomb

City of Gloucester (granted in 1536):

Vert a gold pale and two horseshoes, each between three horsenails, with the state sword of the city surmounted by the swordbearer's hat upon the pale and a chief party gold and purple with a boar's head silver and a red rose and a white one each halved with a gold sun (fig. 139).

Thomas Thirlby, bishop of Westminster, 1540–50:

Gules a cheveron silver and three swans with five lozenges gules upon the cheveron and a chief gold with three slipped daisies (fig. 140).

George Day, bishop of Chichester, 1543–51:

Quarterly silver and gules a cross quartered and counter-coloured and four rayed half-roses counter-coloured with a stalked daisy upon the cross (fig. 141).

Trinity College, Cambridge, 1546:

Fig. 142.
Trinity College,
Cambridge

Silver a cheveron gules and three red roses and a chief gules with a gold leopard and two gold books upon the chief (fig. 142).

Concurrently with the invention of such elaborate arms many others of quite simple character were likewise granted, but the overcrowded shield was nevertheless a distinctly new and characteristic feature of the time.

With the incoming of the Renaissance the artistic applications of heraldry underwent a change, and though survivals here and there may be noted, armorial displays henceforth became more and more restricted to chimney-pieces, firebacks, and monuments, or to panels over the house door or porch. This falling off of the quality of architectural and ornamental heraldry after 1550 is accompanied by a continuance of the output of overcrowded and elaborate shields, which may perhaps be said to have reached a climax when such arms as the following could be granted in January 1560–1 to Doctor John Caius:

Golde semyd wth flowre gentle in the myddle of the cheyfe, sengrene resting uppon the heades of ij serpentes in pale, their tayles knytte to gether, all in proper color, resting uppon a square marble stone vert, betwene theire brestes a boke sable, garnyshed gewles, buckles gold,... betokening by the boke lerning: by the ij serpentes resting upon the square marble stone, wisdom with grace founded & stayed upon vertues stable stone: by sengrene & flower gentle, immortality y[t] never shall fade, &c.

Another typical grant of the same sort of arms was made in 1561 to William Downham, bishop of Chester, 1561–77:

Azure a cheveron silver with two doves with red beaks and legs in the chief and a wolf's head rased silver in the foot with a red rose between two books of the Old and New Testament gules with gold clasps upon the cheveron.

In the same year, 1561, the Company of Barbours and Chirurgeons of London was granted these arms:

Paly argent and vert on a pale gules a lyon passant gardant golde betweene two Spatters argent on eche a double rose gules and argent crowned golde.

In 1569 a new grant was made to the Company by the three kings-of-arms in these terms:

Quarterly the first sables a Cheveron betweene three flewmes argent: the seconde quarter per pale argent and vert on a Spatter of the first, a double Rose gules and argent crowned golde: the third quarter as the seconde and the fourth as the first: Over all on a Crosse gules a lyon passant gardant golde.

A final example of this class must be the arms granted in 1570 to Richard Barnes, bishop of Carlisle:

Azure a bend silver and two gold stars with a black bear spattered with red stars and looking at a black child upon the bend and a chief gold with three red roses rayed.

After 1570, for some occult reason, there was for a considerable time a marked reversion in grants to arms of simpler character and better taste, such as the arms granted by Robert Cooke, Clarenceux, in 1572 to the University of Cambridge (fig. 143), which were: 'Gules a cross ermine and four gold leopards with a book gules upon the cross'; or those granted in 1593 to Richard Brownlowe: 'Gold a scutcheon and an orle of martlets sable.'

Fig. 143.
Cambridge
University

CHAPTER X

HERALDRY IN THE SEVENTEENTH, EIGHTEENTH & NINETEENTH CENTURIES

DURING the first half of the seventeenth century the application of heraldry to buildings and monuments continued to decline, but the official grants of arms maintained the late Elizabethan standard. Strange to say, heraldry did not cease to flourish under the Commonwealth, and the republican successors of the deposed royalist kings-of-arms from time to time issued grants of quite good character. It is curious to note, too, that although the royal arms disappeared with the Monarchy in 1648, the State forthwith adopted the cross of St George as the arms of England, and a harp for Ireland. To these there was added later the cross of St Andrew for Scotland. In 1655 a new great seal for the Commonwealth, designed and engraved by Simon, came into use, and on this there appears a new national shield of arms, with St George's cross in the first and fourth quarters, St Andrew's cross in the second, and the Irish harp in the third, with the lion of Oliver Cromwell on a scutcheon of pretence. Oddly enough this shield is supported by a lion with a royal crown and by a dragon, and surmounted by a helm and mantling with a royal crown and the crowned-leopard crest above.

The post-Restoration heraldry of the seventeenth century and that of the eighteenth century do not call for any special remark; the monumental part of it being mostly dull and lifeless, and the grants of arms continuing to follow the late Elizabethan and Stewart precedent.

It should be noted that in nearly every case grants of arms include that of a crest also; grants of crests alone are also met with. These crests do not as a rule infringe the condition that they, or models of them, could be worn upon a helm, and they of course vary as greatly in character as do those of the fourteenth and fifteenth centuries; but it is as difficult to classify them as it is unnecessary to quote examples.

The final degradation of heraldry is to be seen in the arms and crests granted during the nineteenth century to the sailors and soldiers who distinguished themselves in the great fights at sea and on land with which they were concerned.

Here, for example, are the arms granted to Horatio lord Nelson in 1801, as blazoned in the peerages:

Or a cross patonce sable a bend gules surmounted by another engrailed of the field charged with three bombs fired proper; on a chief of honourable augmentation undulated argent waves of the sea from which a palm tree issuant between a disabled ship on the dexter and a battery in ruins on the sinister all proper.

Lord Camperdown, a few years earlier, was granted arms of like character:

Gules in chief between two cinquefoils (for augmentation) in the centre chief point a naval crown or pendent therefrom by a riband argent and azure a representation of the gold medal conferred upon the first Viscount by George III for the victory off Camperdown thereon two figures the emblem of Victory alighting on the prow of an antique vessell and crowning Britannia with a wreath of laurel below the medal the word CAMPERDOWN and a bugle horn in base argent stringed and garnished azure.

The following is the blazon given by one authority of the arms and crest which were granted, with supporters, to Viscount Exmouth in 1817:

Gules a lion passant gardant in chief two civic wreaths or; and for augmentation on a chief wavy argent in front of a city intended to represent that of Algiers a range of batteries flanked on the sinister by a circular fortified castle with triple battlements proper thereon two flags displayed the one barry wavy or and gules (indicative of the presence of the Bey of Algiers within the said castle) and the other of the last, on the dexter and abreast of the said batteries a ship of the line bearing the flag of an admiral of the blue squadron moored also proper;

with this crest:

the bow of a ship with parts of the pennant and bowsprit standing and appearing as a wreck on a rock the waves breaking round her proper.

Lord Vivian was granted, about 1841, another such crest:

Out of waves a bridge embattled issuant therefrom a demi-hussar of the 18th Regiment holding in his right hand a sabre and in his left a pennon gules inscribed in gold letters CROIX D'ORADE.

These, too, are the arms assigned, according to the peerages, to rear-admiral Sir David Milne, who died in 1845:

Erminois a cross moline quarterly pierced or between three mullets two and one azure a chief of honourable augmentation wavy argent thereon a fortified circular lighthouse with a red flag flying flanked on the dexter by a hexagon battery of three tiers of guns with a like flag flying and on the sinister by another battery of two tiers of guns connected by a wall with the lighthouse, all proper, the whole intended to represent that part of the walls defending the town and port of Algiers to which His Majesty's ship 'Impregnable' which bore the flag of the said rear-admiral was opposed in the said memorable attack on the 27th day of August 1816.

Passing over a number of similar compositions granted at intervals during the century, there may be quoted the arms assigned to Lord Kitchener in 1898:

Gules a chevron argent surmounted by another azure between three bustards proper in the centre point a bezant and over all as an honourable augmentation on a pile or two flagstaffs saltirewise, flowing to the dexter the Union flag of Great Britain and Ireland, and to the sinister a representation of the Egyptian flag all proper, enfiled by a mural crown gules, the rim inscribed KHARTOUM in letters of gold.

The following also appeared in *The Times* so recently as 1912:

The armorial bearings for the Commonwealth of Australia authorized by Royal Warrant dated May 7, 1908, and recorded in the College of

Arms, have now been altered. These arms, of which we published a drawing on August 1, 1908, were:

ARMS. Azure; on an inescutcheon argent upon a cross of St George cottised of the field, five six-pointed stars of the second (representing the constellation of the Southern Cross), all within an orle of inescutcheons of the second, each charged with a chevron gules.

CREST. On a wreath of the colours, a seven-pointed star or.

SUPPORTERS. On a compartment of grass, to the dexter a kangaroo, to the sinister an emu, both proper.

MOTTO. 'Advance Australia'.

This coat, though substantially designed by the Commonwealth Government, was objected to for various reasons in Australia and elsewhere. By a Royal Warrant dated September 19, 1912, which has just been recorded at the College of Arms, the following armorial ensigns were substituted:

ARMS. Quarterly of six; the first quarter argent a cross gules charged with a lion passant guardant between on each limb a mullet of eight points or; the second azure five mullets, one of eight, two of seven, one of six, and one of five points of the first (representing the constellation of the Southern Cross) ensigned with an Imperial Crown proper; the third of the first, a Maltese cross of the fourth surmounted by a like Imperial Crown; the fourth of the third on a perch wreathed vert and gules and an Australian piping shrike displayed also proper; the fifth also or a swan naiant to the sinister sable; the last of the first a lion passant of the second, the whole within a bordure ermine.

CREST. On a wreath or and azure a seven-pointed star or.

SUPPORTERS. Dexter a kangaroo, sinister an emu, both proper.

CHAPTER XI

HERALDIC NOMENCLATURE

IT will probably be allowed that the obscurity of heraldic language could not be illustrated by a better example than that quoted at the end of the preceding chapter; and it is equally certain that what deters so many people from the study of heraldry is the mystifying blazon in which even the officials of to-day wrap up the description of quite simple arms.

Now heraldic language has not always been mystifying. That of the early rolls and records is quite clear, and when it began to be translated out of French into English in the fifteenth century it was equally easy to understand. It was owing to the decadence of heraldry during the Tudor period that the Elizabethan heralds, most of whom cared little and understood less about the subject, began to mask their ignorance with a needless elaboration of heraldic nomenclature which has been in vogue ever since. This terrifying jargon is not only unnecessary, but it can easily be replaced by simple terms. Take for example the arms granted to the Commonwealth of Australia. These could be expressed as correctly heraldically, and in half as many words, as follows:

Six pieces: 1. silver a cross gules with a leopard and four molets gold; 2. azure the constellation of the Southern Cross with an imperial crown in the chief; 3. silver a Maltese cross azure crowned imperially; 4. gold an Australian piping shrike splayed upon a perch wreathed vert and gules; 5. gold a black swan swimming towards the right; 6. silver a lion walking gules: all within a border ermine.

To justify such a blazon as this, and to show how it may properly and logically be used to-day, the language of the early heraldry must be considered, and a beginning may be made upon that of the Great Roll.

When an ordinary is placed between charges or other ordinaries, the roll declares this by simply using the word 'and'; for example:

de argent a une fesse de goules e iij papingais de vert (fig. 144).
de goulys a un cheveron e iij eskallops de argent.
de sable a une cross e iiij cressauns de argent (fig. 145).
de argent a une fesse e ij barres gimyles de goules.
de argent a une fesse e ij cheverons de goules.

Fig. 144. Twenge   Fig. 145. Bernham

Fig. 146. De la Mare   Fig. 147. Cobham

When charges are placed upon an ordinary, 'and' is again used, and with equal clearness, since the rule against colour on colour, or metal upon metal, shows plainly what is meant. Thus:

de argent a une bende de azure e iij egles de or (fig. 146).
de argent a une crois de goules e v flures de or.
de goules a un cheveron de or a iij flures de azure (fig. 147).

Sometimes the place of the charges is more particularly indicated. For example:

de goules a une crois de argent et v moles de sable en la crois.
de or a une bende de sable en la bende iij daufins de argent.

The addition of a label is also noted by 'and':

de goules a une crois patee de or e un label de sable.

To mark the addition of a border or chief, 'with' (*od*) was used:

de argent a un cheveron de goules od la bordure sable besante de or (fig. 148).

de azure frette de argent od le chef de argent (fig. 149).

de or od le chef de sable a ij moles de argent percees (fig. 150).

Fig. 148. Peche   Fig. 149. Holteby   Fig. 150. Gentil

Fig. 151. Pycot   Fig. 152. Sindlesham

In this last example, which is typical of many such, there is no question as to the place of the molets.

Charges that are 'in chief' are always plainly so described:

de azure a ij barres de or en le chef iij rondels de or (fig. 151).

When both field and ordinary were charged, the fact is stated by such a blazon as:

de argent a une fesse e iij escalops de goules en la fesse iij merelos de or (fig. 152).

In the Boroughbridge Roll, which is a little later than the

Great Roll, the descriptions are marked by a frequent use of 'with' (*ove*), e.g.:

dargent ove ij barres de gules ove iij pelotz de gules en chiefe ove un bordure endente de sable.

de gules ove j bende dargent ove iij croiz pate de sable.

The usual formula of the Stacy-Grimaldi Roll, which also dates from early in the fourteenth century, is:

Conan de Ask port dor ove trois barres dazure.

Richard Oysell port dargent ove une sautour engrelee et quatre choughes de cornewaille de sable;

but charged ordinaries take this form:

Robert Ingram port de Ermyne une fess de goules et trois cokels dor en le fees.

Roald de Burgh port dargent ove un sautour de sable et syncque cignes dargent en le sautour.

Rauf de Camoys porte dor ove chief de gules et trois torteaux dargent en le chief.

The heraldic language of the latter part of the fourteenth century, as shown by a few grants, shows no change; and the arms assigned by King Richard II to John de Kyngeston in 1389 are blazoned as 'dargent ove un Chapewe dazur ovesque une plume dostrich de goules'.

Many of the more important royal grants, both in the fourteenth and the fifteenth century, following the language of the grants themselves, describe the arms in Latin, but French continued to be the official language throughout the first half of the fifteenth century.

From at least 1443 onwards French was to a large extent displaced by English, and the blazons of the arms are also in that tongue. Typical examples are:

1443 John Kendal. 'Gowles iij egles of gold betwene a feesche chekke of gold and asure.'

1445–6 John Oxinden. 'Sylver iij oxen sabull armyd with gooldys a cheveryn of the same.'

1451 Barbers' Company of London. 'a felde sabull a cheveron bytweene iij flemys of silver.'

1455 Ironmongers' Company of London. 'silver a Cheveron of Gowles sette bytwene three Gaddes of stele of Asure on the Cheveron three swevells of golde with two lizardes of thiere own kynde (i.e. *proper*) encoupeled with Gowlys on the helmet.'

1466 Carpenters' Company of London. 'a felde Silver a Cheveron sable grayled iij Compas of the same.'

1477–8. Robert, Thomas, and John Gyggs. 'Sable a fret ermyn a chefe chekke silver and of the felde.'

1482. Thomas Northland. 'Silver betwene iij lyonseux · upon a Cheveron Sable · iij · besauntes, The creast upon the helme half a lyon sable sett withunne a wrethe goold and gowles. The mantel Sable furred with hermyn.'

1485. Wax-Chandlers' Company of London. 'Asur thre morteres royal gold upon a Cheveron silver thre Roses goules seded golde. The creste upon the helme a mayden knelyng a monges dyvers ffloures in a Surcote cloth of gold ffurred with ermyn making a garlond being in her hand of the same ffloures sett withinne a wreth gold and goules. The mantell Asur furred wt ermyn.'

These examples show that certain technical terms, like the names of the ordinaries, continue in their old form, as well as the names of the colours, but *or* and *argent* have become 'gold' and silver', and other words have been simply translated.

Another point to be noted is the beginning of the practice now become chronic, of describing the contents of the shield in wrong order. Thus the Kendal arms might more properly have run: 'gowles a feesche chekke of gold and asure and iij egles of gold', and the Northland arms as: 'silver a cheveron and iij. lyonseux sable with iij. besauntes on the cheveron'; and similarly with the Oxinden and Wax Chandlers' arms. This would have been a following of the more logical order of the rolls, which almost invariably blazon the charges after the ordinary. By this means, too, the differencing of arms through added features is made plain. Thus the Great Roll has such cases as:

Sire Thomas de Fornival de argent a une bende e vj merelos de gules.

Sir Robert de Wadesle de argent a une bende e vj merelose de gules
en la bende iij escallops dor.

Modern usage would describe the Furnival arms as 'a
bend between six martlets' and the Wadsley arms as 'on
a bend between six martlets three escallops'; thus empha-
sizing the scallops added for difference instead of the bend
on which they are placed. The Northland blazon similarly
exalts the minor besants above the more prominent lioncels.

The use of English as the language of grants has now been
practically constant, but for some obscure reason the heralds
have reverted to *or* and *argent* for gold and silver. *Argent* began
to be used again for silver, and commonly with it, from 1559
onwards, and *or* for gold about 1590; but Camden and Segar
in the seventeenth century continued the English forms.

Two other usages have also become current. In the older
documents there is never any hesitation in repeating the
name of a colour or a metal, and so late as 1561 a king-of-
arms did not scruple to issue a grant in these terms:

Paly argent and vert on a pale gules a lyon passant gardant golde
betweene two Spatters argent on eche a double rose gules and argent
crowned golde.

To avoid repetition the latter part of this blazon would
probably now run 'between two spatters of the first on each
a double rose of the third and of the first crowned of the
fourth'. To follow such blazons as this, or that of the grant
to the Commonwealth of Australia, one must actually begin
by writing down the colours in order before being able to
interpret 'of the second', 'of the fourth', etc., which is of
course absurd. Yet such wording began quite early. The
expression 'of the felde' occurs in a grant of 1477–8 cited
above, and crops up again constantly in the sixteenth
century. The use of 'of the first', 'of the second', can like-

wise be found in a grant of 1558 by William Hervey, Clarenceux: 'partye per Cheveron sables and argent a Lyon passant in chiefe of the second the point gowtey off the firste'.

Since the Tudor period a large number of other terms have been invented, familiar enough to those whom heraldry concerns, but not in the least 'understanded of the people'. Now there is nothing to be gained by clinging to such terms or to the cumbrous official blazon, when the same things can be described heraldically equally well and more plainly in ordinary language, and if heraldry is ever to become popular the time has come for reformation. The matter can perhaps best be put on a practical basis by following the old English ways of blazoning arms.

Begin by stating the metal, colour, or fur of the field, or whether it is barry, paly, checky, and so forth.

Describe simple charges shortly in plain English and do not trouble about technical terms. There is no need to describe three running dogs, or three fish swimming, as 'in pale', when they are always drawn one above another, or to state that three tripping stags or three roses are '2 and 1', or ten besants or six fleurs-de-lis are '4, 3, 2, 1', or '3, 2, 1'.

If there be a principal ordinary like a pale, fesse, or cheveron, name it after the field, and if it has charges about it, begin the description of these with 'and': e.g. 'azure a fesse and three eagles gold'.

Should an ordinary itself be charged, use 'with' or 'and' as the linking word and add 'on the fesse', 'on the cross', etc. as the case may be. For example:

Barry of six pieces silver and sable with a bend gules and three gold fleurs-de-lis on the bend.

Gules a cheveron gold with three scallops sable on the cheveron.

Ermine a fesse and three eagles vert with three besants on the fesse.

Silver a cross sable and four roses gules with five silver lilies on the cross.

Add 'in' or 'within' if there be a border, and if a label, 'and' or 'with'. For example: Gold a cheveron gules in a border sable with a label azure.

Do not hesitate to repeat the colour or metal, or the number of charges, but do not say 'of the field', 'of the second', or 'as many' roses.

In blazoning animals instead of

accosted		side by side
addorsed		back to back
attired		with horns
couchant		lying down
courant		running or galloping
dormant	say	sleeping
regardant		looking backwards
respectant		facing each other
salient		leaping
sejant		sitting
statant, or		standing
vulned		wounded

Do not say 'ducally gorged', or 'gorged with a ducal coronet (or collar)'; even the Elizabethan heralds authorize the plainer use of 'with a crown (or collar) about his neck'. Chains or lines were often attached to such crowns or collars.

There is no need for retaining the word 'proper' for a charge 'in his proper colour', as the late Tudor heralds liked it, or 'of theire owne kynde' as an earlier grant has it, when there is no doubt about the natural colour of a popinjay, a peacock, or a chough, or of an Australian piping shrike, a kangaroo, or an emu.

Certain time-honoured conventions may be borne in mind. 'A ramping and a roaring lion' as the psalmist calls him, aptly describes the characteristic attitude of the king of beasts, and the old heralds then called him simply 'a lion' and only occasionally 'a lion rampant'. He has an open mouth, and shows his teeth, and has a red tongue and claws; but if painted on anything red, the tongue and claws then become blue. A lion is sometimes sleeping, lying down, walking, or leaping, in which case he must be so described; but his normal aspect is ramping across the shield and looking before him.

When a lion, instead of being side-faced, looks out of the shield full-faced, he becomes heraldically 'a leopard'; not the spotted beast of that name, but merely a lion who looks at you. The leopard is sometimes 'rampant' like a lion, but his characteristic attitude is passant or walking with cat-like tread, full-faced, and it is then enough to call him 'a leopard'. The old blazon of the arms of the King of England was 'gules three leopards of gold', and not 'lions passant gardant in pale'. The 'lion's face' of some of the books is of course 'a leopard's head'. A lion was often shown 'with a forked tail', which was sometimes likewise knotted, as in several instances in the Great Roll.

The normal attitude of horses and bulls, boars, sheep and goats, is standing or walking, while the deer tribe are usually 'tripping' along. Running deer are also to be met with; also running greyhounds and galloping colts or horses.

As with lions and leopards, the tongues and claws of beasts of prey are generally red or blue; while the horns and hoofs of other creatures are often gilded. Stags and bulls need not be described as 'armed' or 'attired' nor full-faced heads called 'caboshed'. A head shown sideways is either torn off or 'rased', or 'cut off at the neck'.

The king of birds with the old heralds was simply 'an eagle', and he was always drawn erect and with wings, tail, and feet spread out so as to cover as much space as possible. Sometimes he was then called a splayed eagle, and also drawn with two heads. 'A pelican' was always drawn 'billing her breast' to draw blood to feed her young, but if standing over them in the nest she was 'a pelican in her piety'. Similarly a peacock with his tail spread out came to be described as 'in his pride'.

Birds other than eagles are usually 'with folded wings' when standing or swimming, but open when 'rising' from the ground, and of course when 'flying'. There is no need to describe them as 'close', 'naiant', or 'volant'.

Butterflies and bats are always shown with their wings splayed.

Fishes are generally 'swimming' one above another; or 'breathing', that is, rising perpendicularly to the top of the water as if for air, in which case they are drawn side by side as in the punning arms of the Lucys. The modern heralds call this supposed breathing 'haurient'.

Snakes or serpents are shown gliding along; also at rest and 'coiled' or 'knotted' as in the Cavendish crest. Frogs and toads and crawling snails occur in late heraldry.

Of fabulous creatures the mermaid was borne quite early as a badge by the Berkeleys; and the wiver and the griffin, delightful winged and long-tailed dragons with two and four legs respectively, were also early favourites. The fierce aspect of the wiver led to his adoption as one of the first animal crests, and the griffin was quite as soon painted upon shields. His normal form was ramping like a lion, pawing the air and with his wings raised behind him. In this position he is sometimes called 'segreant', but needlessly, since a qualifying word is wanted only when he is shown walking.

Two other queer creatures, the cockatrice and the basilisk, are to be found in later heraldry.

A growing tree is ordinarily with leaves, but may be 'with acorns' if an oak, or 'with grapes' if a vine. The books like to say 'fructed'.

A woodstock or tree stump, or a tree torn up by the roots, should be so called.

Certain flowers like roses and daisies are shown without stalks (fig. 153), while lilies, and some leaves like trefoils, normally have short stalks. These need not be called 'slipped' since that applies to flowers that have been plucked with their stalks, like a rose with its leaves, or to a branch that has been torn off a plant or tree.

Fig. 153. Darcy (*Silver three red roses*)

Fig. 154. Gobioun (*A bend and two waxing moons*)

Fig. 155. A star

Fig. 156. A rowel

The sun in his splendour need only be 'a sun'. The moon is generally a 'crescent' with horns upwards; but if shown sideways it is a 'waxing' or a 'waning' moon according as its horns face to the dexter or the sinister (fig. 154), and not the 'increscent' or 'decrescent' moon of the books. Stars (which need not be called 'estoiles') are usually drawn with six or eight rays, either wavy, or alternatively wavy and straight-sided (fig. 155). A comet or blazing star may be found in late heraldry.

A molet (incorrectly spelt mullet) is a star, usually of five points, all straight-sided. When pierced with a round hole it is a rowel (fig. 156).

The confusion between lozenges and mascles in early blazons may be settled by calling a 'lozenge' the form now known as such, and describing the mascle as a false- or voided-lozenge, for which there is ancient precedent. This will get rid of the word mascle.

Fig. 157. St George

As regards the cross, heraldic writers have gone mad, and from the few simple crosses of pre-Tudor days there have been evolved scores of fantastic forms for which it would be difficult to find instances outside the heraldry books. In the *Glossary of Heraldry*, published in 1847, upwards of fifty varieties are enumerated, and there are other modern works in which they exceed two hundred!

As a matter of fact the forms of crosses that have actually been used are quite few. The simple form seen in the arms of St George (fig. 157) of course comes first, and it is also common with the edges engrailed as borne by the Uffords and others (fig. 39), and sometimes it is of the ragged form, as in the arms of Colchester.

There is also the form which has been variously termed the cross patonce, flory, fleury, and a score of other names. The old heralds knew it by another name altogether. To them it was simply a 'cross paty' because the ends were shaped like paws (*pattes*). Such a cross paty occurs in the arms ascribed to St Edward (fig. 102) and in the well-known arms of Latimer (fig. 158); fifteenth-century writers, however, wrongly derived the term from the Latin *patentum*, 'opening' or 'splayed out'. In consequence of this confusion the name paty was given to the cross otherwise called formy, with splayed arms and flat ends, as in the arms of Chetwode (fig. 161), while the old paty form was called patonce or flory. Other names have been invented, quite unnecessarily, from attempts to specify the various ways in which the medieval artists chose to draw or carve a cross paty.

There is another old form, the so-called cross moline, which has had names piled upon it (fig. 159). It was originally called in French *fer-de-moline*, or in English a 'millrind', and represents the iron bearing fixed in the

Fig. 158. Latimer
(*Gules a cross paty gold*)

Fig. 159. Le Brun
(*Azure a millrind cross gold*)

Fig. 160.
The crosslet

middle of a millstone. The old way of drawing it was a cross with forked ends, which were sometimes coiled round, and it was then called a 'cross recercelée', but it still remained a millrind. It was borne ermine on a red field by Anthony Bek bishop of Durham and patriarch of Jerusalem, and on his death in 1310 there passed to his cathedral church divers vestments *cum una cruce de armis ejusdem intextis quæ dicuntur ferrum molendini*: and on his seal of dignity the bishop is shown wearing a chasuble with this device.

Two other crosses were also used, chiefly for powdering the field of a shield, namely the crosslet and the cross formy. The crosslet (fig. 160) is that with the crossed ends familiar to us in the arms of Beauchamp; but the modern squared form is rarer in old examples than another which has the projections rounded off buttonwise. It was perhaps for this reason that the heraldry books call it a cross 'bottonnée'. The cross formy was a cross with splayed arms and flat ends, as in the arms of Chetwode (fig. 161), but if the ends were squared like a modern crosslet it was called a cross potent.

Both the crosslet and the cross formy sometimes had a spiked foot, and were then described as fitchy, because they

Fig. 161. Chetwode (*Quarterly silver and gules four crosses formy countercoloured*)

Fig. 162. A crosslet fitchy

Fig. 163. Siward (*Sable a silver cross flowered at the ends*)

Fig. 164. The tau or St Anthony's cross

could be fixed in the ground (fig. 162). There are also ancient examples of a cross formy sprouting with fleurs-de-lis. This was apparently the cross 'flowered at the ends' of the early rolls, which has come to be called wrongly a cross fleury (fig. 163). A few other early forms, like the tau or St Anthony's cross (fig. 164), and the double-barred cross borne before a patriarch, explain themselves.

There are still very many heraldic words that can be replaced by better. A thing hanging down need not be 'declinant' or 'dejected', or a cross on steps be 'degraded', or a bloody hand 'embrued', or an uprooted tree 'eradicated'. A limb can be 'bent' instead of 'embowed' or 'flexed', and 'cut off' rather than 'couped'. A maiden's head with golden hair should be so described instead of 'crined *or*'. There is also no reason for calling a ring an 'annulet', a star an 'estoile', a sheaf a 'garb', or a paw a 'jamb'; or to burden the memory with names for coloured roundels. Why should a blue roundel be a hurte, a black one an ogress, or a purple one a golpe? 'Roundel azure', 'roundel sable', and 'roundel purpure' are much clearer to the mind and eye. The only roundel with a specific name is the gold one which has always been called a besant, but silver besants occur too in old blazons.

Many other official words can be replaced by better. 'Compony' has an older form in gobony, 'compony-counter-compony' is but checky, 'potent-counter-potent' is only a form of vair, and wavy is quite as expressive as 'undy'. A field or charge powdered with billets, or with drops, or with fleurs-de-lis may surely be so described, in preference to 'replenished with' or 'semy of' billets, etc. or as 'billety', 'gutty', 'fleuretty', or 'fleur-de-lise'. There is no such thing as a bar sinister, and the so-called diminutives are but a modern invention.

In conclusion it will be seen that the grammar of heraldry can be reduced to such simple terms as may be learned without difficulty by anyone, and that there is no need to burden the memory with a vocabulary of unnecessary words, or to continue the cumbrous methods of modern blazonry.

Freed from such shackles, heraldry will appear in quite a different light to the student, who will find that instead of being a dry and repellent subject, it is one full of interest and meaning, and the handmaid of history and art.

CHAPTER XII

THE FURTHER STUDY OF HERALDRY

SINCE the first edition of this book appeared in 1913 so much new work has been done in the heraldic field that the bibliography there given is in great part obsolete, but it remains true, now as always, that those who would pursue further the lines followed in this book cannot do better than consult for themselves the original documents mentioned therein.

Heraldic seals, with heraldry in architecture and on monuments and in painted glass, come first as objects of study, but with them must be read the texts of the rolls of arms and of the earlier grants.

The best general introduction to heraldic seals is a paper by Mr C. H. Hunter Blair, 'Armorials upon English Seals from the Twelfth to the Sixteenth Centuries', in *Archaeologia*, vol. LXXXIX (1943). The fullest account of the rolls of arms is in *A Catalogue of English Medieval Rolls of Arms* by Anthony R. Wagner, published by the Society of Antiquaries, 1950. This contains a general introduction to the subject and lists the existing editions.

The older printed works on heraldry are listed in Thomas Moule's *Bibliotheca Heraldica Magnae Britanniae*, 1822. Later bibliographies are George Gatfield's *Guide to Printed Books and Manuscripts relating to English and Foreign Heraldry and Genealogy*, 1892, the National Art Library, Victoria and Albert Museum: *Classed catalogue of printed books, Heraldry*, 1901, and S. Trehearne Cope's *Heraldry, Flags and Seals: a Select Bibliography, with Annotations, covering the Period 1920 to 1945* (Aslib, 1948). A select bibliography of the subject is also comprised in the article on Heraldry by A. R. Wagner,

H. Stanford London and D. L. Galbreath in the new (1950) edition of Chambers's *Encyclopaedia*, which may also be helpful as a general introduction. Of recent popular works mention may be made of the short introductory essay by A. R. Wagner, *Heraldry in England*, in the King Penguin series, 1946, and the revision by C. W. Scott Giles of Boutell's *Heraldry* (Warne, 1951).

Of somewhat older works special mention may be made of *A Glossary of Heraldry* by J. H. Parker (last edition 1894), *A Treatise on Heraldry British and Foreign* by J. Woodward and G. Burnett, 1892, the article on *Heraldry* by Oswald Barron in the *Encyclopaedia Britannica* (11th edition), and the lively series of papers by him and others in the twelve volumes of *The Ancestor*, 1902–5.

For those who find pictorial heraldry of assistance it may perhaps be pardonable to refer to the volume of coloured facsimiles of the early stall-plates of the Knights of the Garter published by the writer of the present manual in 1901, and to the latest edition of *Heraldry for Craftsmen and Designers* in the 'Artistic Crafts Series of Technical Handbooks'.

Fig. 165. Quartered shield, with a scutcheon of pretence, of the arms of Francis lord Lovel, K.G., *c.* 1483, from his stall-plate

GLOSSARY OF HERALDIC TERMS

Argent silver.

Azure blue.

Bars a number of horizontal bands; the fesse multiplied. Adj. barry. (Fig. 24.)

Baston a narrow bend, either dexter or sinister, lying across the other charges on a shield. (Fig. 52.)

Battled an ordinary with partition line cut in the shape of battlements. (Fig. 41.)

Bend a bend running slantwise from the left-hand corner of a shield; from the right-hand corner it is a bend sinister. Adj. bendy. (Figs. 17, 18.)

Canton formerly the quarter (fig. 31), now a rectangle, less than a quarter, in the dexter chief.

Charges devices to fill in the blank spaces about an ordinary. (E.g. figs. 54, 55.)

Checky a chequered pattern. (Fig. 27.)

Cheveron an ordinary in the shape of a roof gable. Adj. cheveronny. (Figs. 20, 26.)

Chief the head of the shield cut off horizontally. (Fig. 21.)

Cotise a narrow strip, literally 'side-piece', lying parallel to a bend or fesse. (Fig. 51.)

Daunce a fesse zigzagged across the field. Adj. dancetty. (Fig. 53.)

Dexter the left side of the shield (to the beholder).

Engrailed scalloped. (Fig. 39.)

Ermine a conventional representation of the fur, usually white with evenly spaced black tails. (Figs. 5, 143.)

Escutcheon, scutcheon a shield.

Fesse a broad band lying horizontally across the shield. (Fig. 15.)

Field the ground of a shield.

Fretty a pattern of narrow, interlaced bands. (Figs. 86, 149.)

Gemell-bars narrow bars, usually lying parallel to a fesse, but sometimes occurring alone. (Fig. 50.)

Gobony cut into rectangular sections, or gobets. (Fig. 52.)

Gules red.

Gyron triangular piece. Adj. gyronny. (Fig. 29.)

Indented a line broken into a series of pointed teeth. (Fig. 38.)

Invected with rounded notches, the opposite of engrailed. (Fig. 44.)

Lozenge a diamond-shaped device. (Figs. 122, 140.) Adj. lozengy. (Fig. 28.) When voided a lozenge becomes a mascle. Adj. masculy.

Maunche the heraldic sleeve. (Figs. 67, 92.)

Nebuly conventional representation of the edges of a cloud. (Fig. 43.)

Or gold.

Ordinary a general term for the geometrical figures which divide the shield. (Figs. 7 *et seq.*)

Orle a broad band parallel to the edges of the shield. (Fig. 33.)

Pale a broad band lying vertically on the shield. Adj. paly. (Fig. 14.)

Party the vertical division of the shield. Other divisions may be specified, as party fessewise, party bendwise, etc. (Figs. 7–13.)

Pile a wedge-shaped device. Adj. pily. (Figs. 22, 30.)

Proper in natural, not conventional, colour.

Purpure purple.

Quarterly division into four by party and fesse. (Fig. 9.)

Roundel a device of a round form. (Figs. 98, 151.)

Sable black.

Saltire the diagonal, or St Andrew's, cross. (Fig. 19.)

Sinister the right side of the shield (to the beholder).

Tressure a narrow orle, usually flowered. (Figs. 36, 37.)

Vair a conventional heraldic fur. (Fig. 6.)

Vert green.

Voided with the centre cut out. (Fig. 122.)

INDEX

The references are to pages. Arms, devices or terms given in the list of illustrations or the glossary are not entered

www.ingramcontent.com/pod-product-compliance
Ingram Content Group UK Ltd.
Pitfield, Milton Keynes, MK11 3LW, UK
UKHW042147280225
455719UK00001B/156

9 781107 402102